AN EMERALD ODYSSEY

AN EMERALD ODYSSEY

In Search of the Gods
of Golf and Ireland

Paul J. Zingg

Photographs by Eric B. Johnson
(and courtesy of Larry Lambrecht, Pat Ruddy and several golf clubs)

Design by Kathryn E. McCormick
MCCORMICK DESIGN

The
Collins
Press

Published in 2008
by The Collins Press
West Link Park
Doughcloyne
Wilton
Cork

Introduction copyright © Pat Ruddy, 2006
Text copyright © Paul J. Zingg, 2008
Photography copyright © Eric B. Johnson, 2004
Photography copyright © Larry Lambrecht, 1997
and courtesy of:
Photography copyright © Pat Ruddy, 2007; Druids Glen Golf Club, 2004;
The European Club, 2004; Killarney Golf and Fishing Club, 2006; Old Head
Golf Links, 2006; Royal County Down Golf Club, 2006;
Royal Dublin Golf Club, 2004.
Typography by Kathryn E. McCormick, McCormick Design

British Library Cataloguing in Publication Data
Zingg, Paul J. 1947–
An emerald odyssey: in search of the gods of golf and Ireland
1. Zingg, Paul J., 1947– 2. Golf courses – Ireland 3. Golf – Anecdotes
I. Title
796.3'52'09415

ISBN–13: 9781905172566

Printed in Italy by L.E.G.O. S.p.A.

Contents

8   FEATURED & NOTED COURSES

9   FOREWORD: *Pat Ruddy*

13   INTRODUCTION: Gods of Faith and Folk and Fancy

29   ONE: Spirits in the Land

43   TWO: Landscape and Memory

65   THREE: Myth, History and a Sense of Place

81   FOUR: The Broom of Nature

101   FIVE: Gardens of the Gods

119   SIX: Readers of the Game and Gods

139   SEVEN: A Fearful Look: *Kinsale and the Future of Golf in Ireland*

161   EPILOGUE: Why Irish Eyes Are Smiling

173   NOTES

179   SOURCES

191   BIOGRAPHIES & PRODUCTION NOTES

Featured Courses

Ballybunion Golf Club, *County Kerry*
Druids Glen Golf Course, *County Wicklow*
The European Club, *County Wicklow*
The K Club, *County Kildare*
Killarney Golf and Fishing Club, *County Kerry*
Lahinch Golf Club, *County Clare*
Old Head Golf Links, *County Cork*
Portmarnock Golf Club, *County Dublin*
Royal County Down Golf Club, *County Down*
Tralee Golf Club, *County Kerry*
Waterville Golf Links, *County Kerry*

Noted Courses

Adare Manor Golf Club, *County Limerick;* Ashford Castle Golf Club, *County Mayo;* Ballyliffin Golf Club, *County Donegal;* Belvoir Park Golf Club, *County Down;* Carlow Golf Club, *County Carlow;* Carne Golf Club, *County Mayo;* Castlecomer Golf Club, *County Kilkenny;* Ceann Sibeal (Dingle) Golf Club, *County Kerry;* Connemara Golf Club, *County Galway;* Cork Golf Club, *County Cork;* County Sligo (Rosses Point) Golf Club, *County Sligo;* Curragh Golf Club, *County Kildare;* Donegal Golf Club, *County Donegal;* Doonbeg Golf Club, *County Clare;* Dromoland Castle Golf and Country Club, *County Clare;* Druids Heath Golf Club, *County Wicklow;* Enniscorthy Golf Club, *County Wexford;* Enniscrone Golf Club, *County Sligo;* Gort Golf Club, *County Galway;* The Island Golf Club, *County Dublin;* Malone Golf Club, *County Antrim;* Mount Juliet Golf Club, *County Kilkenny;* Portmarnock Golf Links, *County Dublin;* Portsalon Golf Club, *County Donegal;* Portstewart Golf Club, *County Antrim;* Rosapenna Golf Club, *County Donegal;* Royal Belfast Golf Club, *County Down;* Royal Dublin Golf Club, *County Dublin;* Royal Portrush Golf Club, *County Antrim;* St. Margaret's Golf Club, *County Dublin;* Skellig Bay, *County Kerry;* Wicklow Golf Club, *County Wicklow*

Foreword *by Pat Ruddy*

There are those who view golf as a mere sport. Others who use it as a business or social tool. Sad people, these, because they have failed to commune with the spirit of golf and thereby understand it and gain most from it.

To get the most out of golf one has to give the most of oneself to the game and the territory, physical and mental, through which the play transports one.

Just as the breeze fits itself to the shape of the sea and the shape of the land, a golfer's mind must fit into the land shapes, flow with the winds and rejoice in the craggy mental terrain that lies between the first tee and eighteenth green and, yes, between games and throughout life. For life is a mere continuation of golf.

Total absorption is the only state in which the true spiritual and therapeutic values of golf can be realised. A good and lovely golf course helps induce this state, as inspired landforms combine with beautiful backdrops and situations which call upon the inner hero to express himself and soon the transportation existence is shared by all. We are all so close and remain so.

Indian reverence for the dead. Ancient Greek preoccupation with mythological gods. The belief in the Irish fairy and leprechaun. Are they all mad? Or are they just travelling close to the spirit of golf in its very essence?

Golf is not just a ball miraculously skipping across a bunker. It is not just the champion doing, again and again, what no human can do with a long putt. It is communication. Total communication with oneself, within and without, and with the past and the present. It is the power drawn from this communication which empowers the champion and enriches the rest of us.

I am honoured to pen these few thoughts, which should not be crystallised any further except in one's private meditations, for this book in which Paul Zingg plays on the raw edges of our subconscious. He moves towards the central truth and real meaning of our beloved activity. Hopefully, you will enjoy reading him and then taking regular breaks to muse and to enjoy life and golf as never before.

#17, The European Club, County Wicklow

THERE IS A GOLF GOD,

a bunch of them, in fact, and

they are a crafty, nasty lot.

Bob Schieffer, CBS News (1996)

INTRODUCTION

Gods of Faith and Folk and Fancy

Some of the golfing gods are looking down on me the right way.

Tiger Woods, upon winning the 2001 Masters

Completing his second round of play in the 2000 United States Open,

Jack Nicklaus stood in the middle of the eighteenth fairway at Pebble Beach. His booming drive had come to rest in the perfect landing area, just to the left of two pine trees in the right-center of the fairway, leaving him 238 yards to the front of the green. After an encouraging opening round of 73, Jack had struggled throughout Friday's play and now, at thirteen over par, the great champion knew that making the cut for the final 36 holes was not going to happen this year. He faced perhaps the final shots of his career in the Open, a career that spanned six decades and included four championships and four other runner-up finishes in 44 appearances. He was not about to retire meekly.

Turning to his son and caddie, Jackie, he said, 'You know, I haven't tried to knock it on the green here in over twenty years. Let's see if we can knock it on in two today.' Drawing the three wood from his bag, Jack launched a majestic shot through a light afternoon mist, over the seawall and long bunker bordering the left side of the hole, towards the narrow opening of the green. It found the putting surface, only the third ball all day to reach home in two strokes. Watching from the television tower behind the green, Johnny Miller acknowledged the wonderful shot and said, 'The golf gods are smiling on Jack.'

Nicklaus faced a 45-foot putt for his eagle, but stroked it poorly, ending up about 8 feet short of the hole. He now faced a difficult breaking putt for his birdie, or the embarrassing prospect of three-putting his final US Open hole. When Jack's putt stopped on the left edge of the hole, Miller remarked, 'Ah, the golf gods can be cruel.'

A golf magazine, *Maximum Golf*, features a column entitled 'Ask the Golf Gods'. Peering above the masthead of the column and its explanatory note, 'Advice from the ancient game's ornery deities', is a fierce-looking, club-wielding character drawn from central casting of the cartoon world. Lightening bolts flashing behind him, he is part Hercules, part Old Testament. He is Charleton Heston descending Sinai with fire in his eyes, the tablets in his hands, and spectacular hair.

From his headquarters in Sunnyvale, California, 'Reverend' Mark Weeks presides over the World Wide Church of Golf. For $17.93 (plus $3 for shipping and handling) Weeks offers his congregation an official WWCG towel, coffee mug, divot tool, and ball markers. Weeks dispenses these items – and the grace that allegedly accompanies them – with a pastoral blessing, 'May the golf gods be with you.'

A classic 'Peanuts' cartoon contemplates golf's ultimate reward, a hole-in-one, and the influence of the gods. Charlie Brown, caddying for Snoopy, observes: 'I find it strange that the golfing gods have never allowed you to have a hole-in-one. I wonder what that means.' Snoopy considers the observation with one of his own: 'It means we need some new golfing gods.'

The cartoon's creator, Charles Schulz, was an avid golfer and his appreciation of the game matched his love for playing it. Although an ace had not eluded him (he had two, although his first did not come until he was 73 years old in 1996), Schulz understood the joys and frustrations of its quest and the fickleness that seemed to define those who were so blessed to accomplish it. How can solid single-digit handicappers go through their entire golfing lives without one, while others who can barely break 100 have sometimes experienced more than one? Is the answer beyond mortal performance or explanation?

Who, then, might the golf gods be? Are they implorable deities with form and

name? Or are they shapeless spirits, a life force that both animates and mystifies the game? Or are they mere chimeras amusingly conjured to provide some explanation for good fortune and bad?

In whatever manner of appearance or presence, what do they do? Are they fair arbiters of all things about the game? Or are they a tribunal of bodiless hackers who aim to impose their pitiful games on the living? Or are they simply a convenient reminder that we control a lot less about a game we seek to master? Indeed, what designs do they have on the game and those who play it? Why are they assigned a particular fascination with golf? Where do they reside?

'All things are full of gods,' observed Thales of Miletus in the seventh century BC, but it is fairly certain he did not form this opinion while honing his short game in the winds off the Aegean Sea.

A few centuries later, the Roman poet, Ovid, wrote that 'It is expedient that there be gods.' But, again, it is unlikely that the author of *Ars Amatoria (The Art of Love)* reached this conclusion in explaining the fortuitous bounces of his ball in a tight match.

Closer to our century, the British essayist and literary critic Matthew Arnold declared that, 'The seeds of godlike power are in us still.' But there is no record that strong play on a London parkland course, rather than England's course of empire in the Age of Victoria, inspired such a pronouncement.

No, golf obviously was not what linked these men of letters to each other across nearly three millennia. Rather, it was a common fascination with the behaviour of beings, allegedly possessed of supernatural powers and attributes, who seemed to find no human affair unworthy of their attention or irresistible to their influence. These are beings eager as much to torment and beguile as to favour and protect, as interested in victory and defeat on a grand scale as human drama on its most intimate levels. With equal relish and mischief, they observe and effect human behaviour on battlefields and in bedrooms.

If nothing is too great or inconsequential to merit the attention of such beings, why not a game and its pursuit? And why not a game where good and evil, temptation and revelation, godly moments and god awful ones, blend together so seamlessly? Could the gods resist such a toy? No, golf was not what connected a Semitic philosopher of the seventh century BC with an English poet of the nineteenth century AD. But their observations about the interaction between the human and the divine provide a framework to consider the presence and influence of the gods, or more precisely, the forces and spirits that move us to pursue a game. For, if only creations of whimsy, the golf gods find their basis for existence in golf's unique blend of skill and science and chance that makes the game so inscrutable and seductive. It is not unlike the appeal of trying to fathom the unknowable, the very essence of God.

'Whether there are gods or not we cannot say,' wrote Protagoras of Adera in the fifth century BC, 'and life is too short to find out.' This ancient Greek might just as well have asked whether the gods exist as the elements of a deistic belief structure or as metaphor. But either as articles of faith or as ironic inventions, they command attention. And just as the first commandment of the theology of golf is profoundly simple – 'The ball shall be played as it lies' – so, too, is the advice of another venerable one on human reconciliation with godly influence, as deeply believed or tongue-in-cheek as it might be. Said the Roman philosopher-emperor, Marcus Aurelius: 'Live with the gods.'

Spoken like a true Stoic. *Or a golfer.*

Upon winning the 2000 PGA Championship played at the Valhalla Golf Club in Louisville, Kentucky, thus becoming the first player to win consecutive PGA Championships in 63 years and equalling Ben Hogan's 47-year-old standard of three major victories in one year, Tiger Woods explained: 'I felt my game would bring me to the point where I would contend for major championships. *It's up to the golf gods to see if I could get lucky or not.*'

Tiger's victory at Valhalla – a course named after the hall of immortality in Scandinavian mythology into which the souls of the great heroes of battles are received – raises another issue about the golf gods: where do they hang out? Are they more likely to exert their presence at divinely evocative places like the Olympic Club in San Francisco or Olympia Fields in Illinois? Might they have particular influence at The Sanctuary in Sedalia, Colorado, Paradise Valley in Fairfield, California, or Druids Glen in County Wicklow, Ireland? Might they battle for golfing souls at Salem Country Club in Peabody, Massachusetts, or the Devil's Paintbrush Golf Club in Caledon, Ontario? Are Hell Bunker at St Andrews and Hell's Half-Acre at Pine Valley extraordinarily likely settings for the torment of the gods, albeit, fallen ones?

What's in a name, though? Are place names sufficient to suggest godly presence? Or do the gods signal a deeper spirituality, perhaps something that transcends physical space, something fundamental to the beliefs and history of the people who reside where these courses are located? If this is so, might not the very nature and meaning of the game particularly be revealed in a land where the spirit *of* the game and spirits *about* the game exist as vital and

Dolmen, The Burren, County Clare

integral elements not only of its golfing scene, but also of the larger community culture? And might not such a land inspire deep imaginings or influences beyond human comprehension?

With all due respect to the birthplace of the game and Scotland's magnificent sites for its pilgrims – from St Andrews to Southerness, Muirfield to Machrihanish, Dunbar to Dornoch – there is no place where the ensemble of a rich golfing tradition and a deep spiritual dimension in the history of its land and people is more complete than in Ireland. **If the essence of the game is to be found, if its meaning is to be approached, then the Emerald Isle is the place to undertake the search.**

Seeking enlightenment, of course, no more guarantees a successful quest than occasionally exhibiting god-like behaviour merits a place in the Pantheon. Asked about his pairing with Tiger Woods in the final round of the 2000 Players Championship and his gutsy one-shot victory over Woods, Hal Sutton said, 'I do not pray to Tiger. He is not a god.' Woods' friend Michael Jordan, who redefined basketball as much as Tiger has done for golf, agreed, but explained, 'I don't think he's a god, but I believe he was sent by one.' Even so, awed by Tiger's nineteen under par performance that destroyed the field in winning the 2000 Open, Tom Watson, himself a five-time winner of The Open, declared, 'He is something supernatural.'

Again, perhaps. But even those apparently favoured by the gods and destined for greatness can discover harsh lessons on other than their own terms. When Woods suffered an 81, the worst scoring round of his professional career in the third round of the 2002 Open at Muirfield, thus derailing a march to the Grand Slam that many had all but conceded, Michael Bamberger of *Sports Illustrated* provided some perspective: 'There is the real God, there is the accuracy god, and then there are the golfing gods. They had a message for Tiger, and for us, straight from the black Scottish night: Not just yet.' [1]

John Ziegler, a radio talk-show host in Philadelphia, has not been discouraged by Tiger's occasional failures,

including a winless stretch in the majors from the 2002 US Open to the 2005 Masters. Seeking to glorify Tiger's achievements beyond cereal boxes, billboards, and TV ads, he launched on 1 April 2001 – yes, April Fool's Day – tigerwoodsisgod.com, the official website of The First Church of Tiger Woods. Says Ziegler about Tiger's godly credentials, 'We are simply providing the evidence.'

'The gods can never leave a man in the world who is privy to their secrets. They cannot have a spy here,' said Henry David Thoreau. But it seems certain that some players have tapped into the supernal secrets more fully than others, while all players have those moments, however rarely, when they appear to be touched by the divine.

What is god-like behaviour with respect to golf? If perfection

is the answer, can a game that 'cannot be won, only played', as Steven Pressfield, the author of *The Legend of Bagger Vance*, described, offer such? Perhaps no golfer pursued perfection in the game more obsessively than Ben Hogan. But asked whether eighteen under par constituted a perfect round, he coolly explained, 'No, a perfect round would be eighteen.'

Such unattainable perfection invites, then, a less sweeping notion of superhuman performance. Hogan emphasised the nature of golf as perhaps the least perfectible of all games when he admitted that he rarely hit more than a half-dozen shots in a round that performed exactly as he intended. How discouraging this admission must have been to his fellow professionals who often wondered why someone with such a grooved swing needed to practise as hard and as much as he did. 'He was our ideal,' said four-time British Open champion Peter Thomson about Hogan and his habits. 'He was the standard to which we all aspired but none of us ever reached.' And this about a man who only hit a half-dozen shots in a round that were completely satisfying to him!

Hogan's definition of a perfect round underscores the simple eloquence of golf: it is a game of individual elements

#6 Lahinch Golf Club, County Clare

and moments. **Each aspect of the swing, each shot, each hole, is distinctive.** Integrated and connected, to be sure, but requiring focused attention on the shot at hand and the circumstances of the hole it has to negotiate. For Hogan, perfection boiled down to the confident ability to repeat a good swing under any conditions. His 'secret', after which his contemporaries and legions of admirers since have sought, had little to do with his instructional vocabulary – 'supinating' wrists or 'pronating' hands – and even less to do with his austere manner and dress. His secret was his awareness of golf's ultimate simplicity – the exactitudes of focusing on one swing, one shot at a time – and his determination to develop the mental toughness and physical skill to succeed in such a game.

If Hogan's greatest rounds – his six-under par play in the final two rounds at Carnoustie for the 1953 British Open championship, or his 69 in the playoff for the 1950 US Open title at Merion, or his 30 on the back nine in the third round at the 1967 Masters – are only illusions of perfection, then what can be said for all other claims on such performance? Only that the game is not about being perfect. Rather, says sports psychologist Bob Rotella, 'Golf is about how well you accept, respond to, and score with your misses much more so than it is a game of perfect shots.'[2]

So, if perfection is not possible, and if each and every shot is an occasion for us to face this awareness, can it be any wonder why we mortals who play this game imagine a divine horde mixing hope and futility in the course of our rounds? To giveth and taketh. To reveal perfection in one moment, one swing, and to erase it in the very next. *Torment, temptation, attainment, atonement – all within the journey of a single hole.*

The notion of journey, of course, is one that is central to golf. A round of eighteen holes covers a particular landscape. It is a physical outing. But a round also offers the prospect of greater proficiency in the game. It is a learning expedition. What transpires on the journey may not entail the trials of Odysseus, but it does evoke his epic of exile and return. A round of golf, after all, is just that, *a round*. It brings us back to the point of departure, the clubhouse, and it signals the conclusion, however triumphant or miserable, of a player's encounter with the day's challenges and opportunities. On some days of particular struggle, the sight of the clubhouse beyond the eighteenth green is a welcome signal that the day's ordeal is nearly over. On others, though, this sight has a bittersweet appeal. It is reward and regret, the end of the quest and the boundary of pleasure.

That so much can occur within this journey is perhaps golf's most compelling feature. For not only does the game involve a series of connected moments and pathways in the present – the accumulated score on a prescribed landscape – but it also engages the player's memory in rich and troubling ways. Again, for Hogan, the ability to recall and trust the memory of a good swing emphasised the critical relationship between remembrance and performance. Practice contributed to his confidence that he could do this consistently, that is, recall the good shots and bring that memory to bear on the immediate ones.

For the great majority of golfers, though, approaching Hogan's plane of concentration and dedication, much less attaining it, is not very likely. 'Even more than the shot-making process,' observed Dow Finsterwall, who competed against Hogan in the 1940s and 1950s, 'the ability to concentrate is the difference between the club player and the golf professional.' Levels of concentration, of course, also distinguish Hogan, Nicklaus and Woods from their respective contemporaries. Yet, there is no doubt that the expectation – or, at least, the hope – of a good shot is rooted in the experience of being able to produce one. This is the essence of envisioning a golf shot. The trick, of course, is being able to bring to bear in the moment the memory of a good swing, a successful shot, not the recollection of an ugly or failed one.

Eddie Loos, a highly respected American teaching professional, described the mental aspects and demands of golf in this fashion: 'Every game of golf that has ever been played – whether the medal was 68 or 168 – has taken place on a golf course that measured 8 inches or less. I arrived at the dimensions of this golf course by taking a ruler and measuring my own head from back to front.'

If a player's first and greatest challenge is handling the demands of this 'course', then there is little wonder why the game is such a fertile playground for a gallery of the mind's inventions – the golf gods. **For not only can they confuse and amuse with the flight and bounces of the ball, but they can plant such images in the mind's eye forever.** That being the case, how easier said than done it is to sift through the inventory of one's experience and choose images that inspire confidence, not harbour doubt.

'The thing that sets golf apart from the other sports,' said Jack Nicklaus, 'is that it takes self-confidence, an ability to rely totally on yourself.' But, even in his prime, Jack never won more than seven tournaments in a year. 'No one will ever have golf under his thumb,' observed Bobby Jones, the greatest amateur player in the history of the game. 'No round ever will be so good that it could not have been better.' If the game offers neither perfection of play nor mastery of outcome, what assurance exists that its pursuit entails more than merely casting one's fate to the wind?

Enter the gods – or whatever guise they take. *Luck, fate, destiny, karma, kismet – or providence.* 'You seem to forget,' explained Walter Travis when it was suggested to him that he lost the US Amateur in 1902 due to an opponent's luck, 'that luck is a part of the game and a good golfer must be good at all parts of the game.' Could it be that Travis, a three-time winner of the US Amateur and once the British Amateur, and Thales the Greek were saying the same thing – live with luck, live with the gods? For among all the principles in the game, one prevails: you play the course as you find it. Like life, golf is full of breaks. And the true champion accepts this reality in order to face it.

Luck and providence. **No land embraces these elements more fully or sees them more inextricably linked than Ireland.** With equal conviction and fervour, the people of Éire see the hand of Patrick or the luck of the Irish in the blessings they receive and the hardships they endure. It is an outlook that acknowledges both divine will and serendipity with neither sentimentality nor struggle. And it is one that is particularly suited to accepting the fortunes of a game the outcome of which skill alone cannot determine.

Yes, if the golf gods exist, they must be found in this land where golf has taken a special hold and where spirits abide, and comfort, and torment.

We're off to Ireland.

CHAPTER ONE

Spirits in the Land

Kelt, Briton, Roman, Saxon, Dane, and Scot,

time and this island tied a crazy knot.

John Hewitt, *Collected Poems* (1991)

Most of us probably know at least four countrysides in Ireland. Like Caesar we divide our Gaul. But the divisions we make are not geographical. Our four Irelands are lands of the spirit.

Conrad Arensberg, *The Irish Countryman* (1937)

#11, Lahinch Golf Club, County Clare

The golfing scene in Ireland is a magnificent blend of mystery, beauty, and variety that underscores how golf, like no other, is a game that is joined to the land as much as it has been shaped by the land. With almost 400 courses in a country of about 4.3 million people, Ireland has nearly as many courses per capita as Scotland, the celebrated cradle of golf.

Ireland also boasts nearly one quarter of the world's approximately 250 true links courses. These unique settings for the game along the coasts of the Irish Sea and the Atlantic Ocean owe their distinctive features and challenges to no human hand. For what prepared this landscape so fittingly for golf was the shaping power of nature itself – the ancient crumpling of the earth's crust, the many moods of the sea and winds, and the consequences of the great glaciers that moved relentlessly across it over several ice ages. The moraines and eskers, drumlins and erratics, and pitted outwash plains that the moving ice left in its slow processional are the elements of true glacial topography. It is a coarse and obdurate landscape, spectacularly wild and beautiful, kettled and kamed, untillable, inimitable, and irresistable. *Perfect for golf.*

Inland and upland, the pleasures of the game are no less abounding. From the lake country of Killarney to the veiled valleys of the Wicklow Mountains, from the parkland settings of Mount Juliet and Druids Glen to the wooded castle grounds of Adare and Dromoland, Ireland offers something for every golfing taste. It especially offers a manner and pace of play that are universally appealing. 'The game is meant for walkin', declared Agatha McNaughton, one of Michael Murphy's delightful inventions in his classic novel, *Golf in the Kingdom.* And, she added, to do so 'fast'. There is scant evidence at any Irish course that the case could be otherwise. With rare exception, no fleets of canopied golf carts stand at the ready. No black top pathways scar the landscapes for their conveyance. The aesthetic benefits go beyond the deliverance from the sight and sound of buzzing golf buggies stuffed with overweight riders and their equally massive bags racing and braking around the course. Instead, the scene is the game being played as it was meant to be – quickly paced, actively engaged, and truly shared. To recast Mark Twain's demeaning observation, golf **with carts** is a 'good walk spoiled' because the walk never occurred.

Traversing a golf course seated on a cushion bears no resemblance to the game pursued on foot because the essence of golf is human connection to the landscape. That bond is cast in the opportunity to experience the game through unique access to its character and memory. For unlike a seat at Las Ventas, or courtside at Wimbledon, or premium level seats at Croke Park, golf permits its devotees a literal feel for the game and its purest elements. This personalised experience entails more than close inspection of the playing grounds on a stroll across famous acres as a tournament spectator. On public access courses like St Andrews, Pebble Beach, Bethpage, Torrey Pines, Ballybunion, and Lahinch, it includes the opportunity to re-enact shots from the exact locations where history was made. Perhaps the best example of this in the United States is number seventeen at Pebble Beach, where Tom Watson holed a birdie chip from the high greenside rough to win the US Open in 1982. When the flagstick is back left, the usual location for the fourth round of the Open, attempting that shot has become a virtual ritual for anyone playing the hole.

Whether in the recollection of one's own swings and rounds, or awareness of the great shots and performances in the history of the game, golf connects memory and landscape in such an essential and powerful way as to constitute perhaps its most distinctive characteristic. There is a transcendent quality to the game that is not limited to time and place, although proficiency in the game requires an enormous sense of present-mindedness, that is, immediate focus on the shot and situation of the moment. It is a game, in other words, where the spirit *of* the game is as vital to its understanding and enjoyment as the spirits *about* the game. There is promise in exploring the nature and appeal of this game in a land where the memory of past events also clings to certain places and encourages even less sensitive souls to resonate to that memory.

Ireland is such a place – a land of deep spiritual memory and presence.

For long before some ancient striker launched a featherie, or some other object, across the dunes of the beckoning landscape that would eventually reveal itself as the Ballybunion links, much earlier than the founding of Ireland's oldest golf club, Royal Curragh, in 1883, and, surely, well before someone associated a particular community of gods with golf, spirits inhabited the land.

They accompanied – and some say greeted – the land's first human settlers, who most likely arrived from south-west Scotland or Britain in primitive boats about ten thousand years ago. Following the banks of Ireland's rivers and lakes, these Stone Age, or Mesolithic, hunters and food-gatherers led a largely nomadic existence. Their way of life changed very little for several thousand years. Around 4000 BC, however, came the introduction of stone tools and weapons. The most important consequence of this development was the gradual transformation of wandering tribes to sedentary, though isolated, communities based on farming and the domestication of cattle and sheep. Such communities also massed people together, a critical factor for the development of group iden-tity and the construction of defence works and other monumental projects.

The most noteworthy of the latter were a series of stone and earthen passage tombs which both anchored the communities that settled about them and provided a focus for their consideration of the meaning of life and death. Compared to the huts in which these people lived, the great tombs they built were magnificent structures. The mound above the tomb at Newgrange in the broad valley of the River Boyne about 40 miles northwest of Dublin, for example, covers over an acre and required over 200,000 tons of stone and earth in its construction. The awesome scale of these tombs suggested fascination and hope in an afterlife. For with little relief from the harsh conditions of their earthly existence, it is not surprising that a people would depict the 'next' life in grand terms and build impressive portals to the spirit world.

The introduction of metalworking around 2000 BC provided a new tool for spiritual communication. The great tombs gave way to more scalable structures with more refined features. These included cairns, standing stones, and stone circles, often incised with petroglyphs or the simple strokes of an ancient alphabet called *ogham*, named after Ogmios, the Celtic god of literature, who is credited with inventing it. Used for a variety of purposes, including ritualistic practice, quasi-astronomical observation, or simply as signposts and tomb markers, these monuments abound throughout the country and are highly visible reminders of the relationship between cultural development and spiritual expression.

The Irish Neolithic communities also explored identity through story, especially those that helped to explain the mysteries of the land and their relationship to it. Gods figured prominently in these tales. These were not cute deities, ancestors of such fictional golf gods as 'Shank, the God of Cruelty' or ' Twitch, the God of Putting'.[1] These were gods with attitudes and agendas and they governed every aspect of life and death. The war goddesses Badh, Macha, and Niet were not ones to cross; the earth goddesses Echtga, Eithne, and Tailtiu were not ones to ignore. A complex, active pantheon provided meaning for mortals who could not otherwise explain their own existence and purpose.

The arrival of the Celts around 500 BC brought another spiritual layer to Ireland and profoundly influenced the emergence of a distinctive Irish society. A multi-ethnic collection of peoples, the Celts traced their origins to central Europe. Their migrations westward to the Atlantic spread over the course of about a thousand years. Connected through language, art, and a powerful mythology that informed their beliefs and values, the Celts embraced a social order strongly rooted in a warrior code and organisation. The anarchy and violence endemic to Ireland when they arrived served their conquest well and they quickly subjugated the island, although they fought endlessly against each other and various waves of invaders for the next dozen centuries.

Standing stone with spiral and diamond carvings,
Newgrange, County Meath

The polytheistic religion of the Celts, a powerful blend of magic and vision, fear and eternal longing, mirrored and supported their angry existence. Featuring sacred groves, human sacrifice, a severed-head cult, belief in an afterlife, and a learned class of ministers and interpreters called druids, Celtic religion had a highly holistic and integrated quality. It is very hard to distinguish between the Celts' actual history and the activities of their numerous gods and goddesses. In many respects, the world that unfolds through Celtic story and tradition resembles that of the *Iliad* and the *Aeneid*, but there are important differences. The heroes of the Greek and Roman epics are human beings, however divinely harassed or favoured they might be. In Celtic theology, though, the gods and goddesses are more often seen as ancestors rather than as creators, more engaged in human struggle and passion than above them. *All this makes for a lively spiritual culture where godly influence and god-like behaviour are capable of manifesting themselves in ways that make no distinction between what is real and what is imagined.*

Into this strange mix about the fourth century AD came Christianity. The new faith most likely reached Ireland as a consequence of trade and raids on the Roman outposts in Britain. But, within a few generations, largely through the evangelical zeal of St Patrick, who preached the Gospel in the latter half of the fifth century, Christianity had firmly taken hold. Considerably less patrician and episcopalian than its manner and structure in Britain and Western Europe, the Christian Church in Ireland drew its support from alliances with local Celtic chieftains and the monasteries they patronised.

The Celtic-Christian dialogue assured both the growth and distinctiveness of the Irish Church, most notably its fairly tolerant attitude toward the ancient habits of the people it sought to convert. How far below the surface of the old beliefs and devotions the Christian Church ever got is still a matter of controversy. The Church's work to record the laws, annals, and myths of Celtic society often resulted in co-mingling them with Christian themes and images, as the *Book of Durrow* or the *Book of Kells* illustrate. Whether it is possible, or necessary, to draw absolute distinctions among these elements of Irish Christianity is another's task. It is important to emphasise, though, that even the oldest mythic layers in Irish history and culture can be recognised on the surface of the country's contemporary life.

Still other invaders and would-be conquerors came to Ireland's shores many centuries ago. Around 800 BC, Scandinavian pirates initiated a period of raids on the islands and their scattered settlements along the eastern coast. Although striking terror far and wide, the Norsemen especially threatened the Christian Church as they seized some of the most important ecclesiastical centres in the country and desecrated their altars with pagan ceremonies. In the end, though, the Norse failed to extend their power beyond a few fortified ports, including Dublin, Waterford, Wexford, Cork, and Limerick. They were eventually absorbed into the shifting political currents of their neighbours, but their brief dominance left lasting imprints. Their outposts constituted Ireland's first urban settlements and their heathen pantheon, headed by the great god Odin and Thor the Thunderer, slipped into the land's grand mythology.

The Normans came next and ushered in a chain of events that would eventually effect the political and religious divide in Ireland that continues to the present. Having secured power in Britain after their victory over the Saxons at the Battle of Hastings in 1066, the Normans extended their influence and feudal order to Ireland. But, never successful in consolidating their power, they were vulnerable to both Celtic opposition in Ireland and Anglo intrigue in England. A long chapter of conflict, lasting almost three centuries, ensued as English royal authority contended with the great Anglo-Norman houses for political and economic control of Ireland.

Again, a battle on English soil had fateful consequences for Ireland. This time it was the decisive victory of Henry, the Earl of Richmond, over Richard III at Bosworth Field in 1485. The crown of England passed to Henry and the House of Tudor. His successor, Henry VIII, subsequently broke with the Vatican and established himself as the head of the English Church when he did not receive a papal annulment for his first marriage. Although the great majority of Irish remained faithful to the Catholic Church, the establishment of Protestantism as the state religion of England plunged Ireland into an era of religious and political conflict that has yet to run its course.

The long reach of these events reveals how history lives in Ireland, unjettisoned, unforgotten, and, often, unforgiven.

History also lives in Ireland through story, namely, a powerful oral story-telling tradition that supports the rich mythological foundations of Irish culture and identity. Changelings, goblins, merrows, cloven-hoofed pookas, the shape-shifting sidhe, and the headless dullahan mingle with the solemn conjurations of the Christian Church and the incantations of New Age mystics. The acknowledgment of a spirit world reflects a strong sense in Ireland that lives and land are shared with beings other than ourselves.

These notions have been perpetuated for thousands of years and Ireland is certainly not unique in having such themes communicated down through generations and interwoven into personal experience. Like other largely agricultural and rural societies, Ireland can testify to the importance of story and storytellers and the continuity of myth. But, perhaps because Ireland is as much a physical place as a state of mind – especially for those many millions of Irish descent scattered around the world who see Ireland 'as a point of ancestral reference, an island hidden in a cloud'[2] – the old myths have demonstrated remarkable resistance to the numbing, homogenising influence of television and mass consumerism.

For somehow among the physical ruins of a violent history that 'make a ghostly quarter to towns',[3] the image of the buffoonish 'stage Irishman', the deeds of its saints and scholars, and many other 'Irelands', a basic unity emerges. From the Neolithic deities who abided in the land when Ireland was first inhabited, to the one Christian God and registry of saints who have been invoked by both Catholics and Protestants throughout 'the Troubles', Ireland has been haunted and defined by spiritual influence, especially affecting the relationship of its people to the land. This has been a constant element of Irish history and culture. It has formed a strong thread that has run clearly through Ireland's multiple and connected 'worlds' – Celtic and English, Catholic and Protestant, planter and Gael, loyalist and nationalist, agrarian and urban, civilian and barbarian, Christian and pagan, immigrant and emigrant, ancient and modern, mythic and true.

In short, Ireland 'is an idea with many histories',[4] and a place where the sacred and the supernatural are everywhere in the Irish experience, both on the surface and beneath.

Stone Circle, Kenmare, County Kerry

To experience Ireland is to seek the expressions of these qualities and conditions. They are not hard to find. They are in the conversations of neighbours, the architecture of cities, the words of poets, the songs the Irish sing, the games they play. Golf in Ireland is a window on this world because it is so clearly tied to the game's most compelling and elemental values – a sense of history, respect for the land, and self-discovery. Each have powerful spiritual dimensions that include divine invocation and felt presence. The gods of golf, of course, are not members of the great pantheons of Irish myth or faith, but they are of the culture of golf. Seeking these gods will not yield a unique order of deities, but it can reveal something transcendent in the game they observe and the players who pursue it. Undertaking this search in a land of deep spirituality and presence holds the promise of a successful journey.

The true links were moulded by divine hands.

Robert Hunter, *The Links* (1926)

CHAPTER TWO

Landscape and Memory

Bunker, Royal County Down Golf Club, County Down

In discussing the need for simplicity of design, the chief object of every golf course architect worth his salt is to imitate the beauties of nature so closely as to make his work indistinguishable from nature itself.

Alister MacKenzie, *Golf Architecture* (1920)

In Ireland the past has often seemed to matter more than the future.

The Irish have summoned up to the sessions of silent thought a crowd of witnessing memories.

Ernest Barker, *Ireland in the Last Fifty Years* (1916)

The scene has become increasingly familiar. The Big Name Pro stands on a high point overlooking a grand landscape. What he surveys could be a wooded mountain valley, a seaside sweep of dunes, rolling foothill country, or the high desert. It makes no difference. Like so many explorers depicted in the courthouse murals painted in the 1930s that commemorated the American westward course of empire, he gazes heroically, knowingly, at the country before him. One hand holds a topographic map of the area he views. The other points vaguely to a spot in the distance. A convenient photographer captures the exact moment when the Big Name Pro pronounces, **'I've never seen such a spectacular setting.** God surely intended a golf course to be built here.'

The photo will appear in various brochures and advertisements promoting the course and, often, the gated and pricey residential community surrounding it. The Big Name Pro will not likely show up again at the site until opening day when he will christen the course with a record-setting round and another pronouncement about how proud he is to affix his 'signature' to such a fine layout. He will then move on to another 'unique' and similarly inspired site that he will honour with his name and vision.

Ireland is not exempt from such scenes.

Bernard Langer said that the dune land above the Velvet Strand just south of the picturesque seaside village of Malahide, and only a few miles northeast of Dublin city center, was 'an irresistible place of magic and beauty'. The German champion proclaimed it to be among the 'very few locations in Europe that could have allowed the opportunity and landscape to design a classic championship links'. He is the architect of record for the Portmarnock Golf Links, his first foray into course design, which opened for play in 1995.

Arnold Palmer ordained the cliffs and coastline of Tralee, which initially accommodated play in 1896 on a nine-hole layout, as 'ideally suited for the building of a golf course'. Working with his design group partner, Ed Seay,

Palmer so transformed the original course in the early 1980s that even Arnie's enthusiasm for the site was eclipsed by others. The noted British golf writer, Peter Dobereiner, for example, was so enthralled with what he discovered in the dunes above the broad Banna Strand, where parts of *Ryan's Daughter* were filmed, that he wrote: 'Robert Louis Stevenson got it all wrong when he described the Monterey Peninsula as the finest conjunction of land and sea this earth has to offer. As a spectacle, Tralee is in a different class.' Tralee's scorecard credits the course as **'Created by God, Designed by Arnold Palmer.'**

Greg Norman's first foray into course design in Ireland focused on a remote, windswept stretch of dunes terrain overlooking Doughmore Bay in the tiny western County Clare village of Doonbeg. Identified by the Scottish Black Watch Regiment stationed in Limerick in 1891 as perfect grounds for a course, the site was never developed because of its inaccessibility. Instead, the Scots turned their attention to Lahinch, about twenty-five miles up the coast and conveniently situated on a rail line. Norman, however, was not deterred by the location. 'I've got the best site you've ever seen at Doonbeg in Ireland,' he gushed. Declaring himself to be 'the luckiest designer in the world because of the uniqueness of this site', he explained that 'you do not get too many opportunities to work on a piece of land like this'.[1] With Norman's assurances that the course will not be 'Americanised', Doonbeg opened for play in the summer of 2002 to rave reviews.

The pros do not have a monopoly on hyperbole. Joe Carr, Ireland's greatest amateur champion, was part of the design and development team that planted a golf course on top of the Old Head peninsula on the southern coast of County Cork.[2] He proudly cited one observer's opinion of what he and the others involved in this project achieved: **'If God were going to play golf, he would definitely pick the Old Head of Kinsale as his home course.'**[3]

A slight variation of the Big Name Pro is the World Famous Architect. There was none more famous or prolific than Robert Trent Jones, Sr, whose designs, such as Spyglass, Valderrama, and Congressional, have earned world-wide acclaim and frequent listing on most 'must play' lists. At age 74, he was invited to lay out a new course among the spectacular dunes immediately adjacent to the venerable Old Course at Ballybunion. 'I was given a once-in-a-lifetime opportunity,' he said about the Cashen Course, which opened in 1984. 'The property I had to work with is perhaps the finest piece of links land in the world ... an outrageously beautiful stretch of God-given land.'

Whether or not Ireland's great links courses were inspired by divine visitation or direction, we'll probably never know. But one point is certain about them: **they were revealed within the land rather than imposed upon it**. As such, they are much more a manifestation of forces beyond human hand than what the shaping power of bulldozers and backhoes could possibly accomplish.

The *ur*-model, of course, for such a site is the Old Course at St Andrews, Scotland. Notwithstanding his pro-prietary praise for Old Head and its apparent appeal to the Almighty, even Joe Carr pointed to the Old Course as the place where he would play for the rest of his life if he had to choose just one course. It is important, then, to understand what is so special about the playing grounds of the Royal and Ancient Golf Club in order to appreciate its influence and the attempts – however artificial and futile, yet persistent – to capture its magic elsewhere.

When Sam Snead first saw the heaving sea of dunes, bunkers, and gorse from his train window as he travelled to St Andrews for The Open in 1946, he thought he was looking at an old, abandoned golf course, long gone to seed. Sam's initial reaction has been shared by many others, who perhaps expected to behold something more obviously grand, or, at least, something announced more grandly. But there are no arched entranceways to the course, no shrubbery arranged to spell out 'The Old Course', no high walls with 'No trespassing' signs surrounding it. It sits as it has for about four hundred years, resting patiently, bewitchingly, unassumingly between the sea and the town.

For most golfers, certainly those whose playing experiences do not regularly include true links courses, St Andrews is a far cry from the industrially-reproduced acres that accommodate their normal rounds. The charm of the Old Course and links land courses generally, as Donald Ross explained, lay in distinct environmental and natural attractions that contribute to their overall 'fitness' for, and harmony with, the Scottish game.[4] These are golfing grounds which, for the most part, have not been transformed from something else. The pure savagery of the land and the circumstances of wind and sea that continue to shape it effect a kind of eloquence and appeal that are finite and transcendent. On one hand, the course evokes the memory of human interaction on it, that is, the play of centuries and the great moments within the history of the game that have occurred here. On the other, St Andrews provides a spiritual bond for players everywhere, a sense of connection through time and space. As both unique sporting artifact and living theatre, especially when its time on The Open rota occurs, the Old Course has had a cult of exceptionalism develop about it.

There is no course anywhere that possesses the elements – history, character, setting – that distinguish the Old Course at St Andrews. Claims to such, like copying its famous holes or hazards or building replicas of the Swilken

View of the Long Strand below the seaside holes #15 and #16,
Tralee Golf Club, County Kerry

Bridge or borrowing its name, are preposterous for they fail to recognise that the spirit of St Andrews is an entire golfing ensemble and culture, including the town, that cannot be reproduced. Rather than seek to copy St Andrews, it is better to consider what it represents and how it was formed. For within this appreciation of greatness are echoes of the Old Course that can be recognised elsewhere, especially a glimpse into the game's past and a clue to the game's very nature.

Foremost among these elements are its mysterious origins, telluric identity, and variety of play, the latter especially as affected by the weather. Combined with the exhilaration that accompanies the attempt to master the geometry and geography of the game, these are the same elements that characterise each of Ireland's three most renowned courses in terms of international reputation and ranking – the Old Course at Ballybunion, Portmarnock, and Royal County Down. Not surprisingly, these are qualities that evoke both mythic and supernal references.

Although they are situated in very different parts of Ireland, these three courses evolved in similar ways. The oldest among them as an established club is Royal County Down which was founded in 1889 at the beach resort town of Newcastle, Northern Ireland, by members of the Belfast Chamber of Commerce. A direct rail link between Belfast and Newcastle provided the golfers of the Chamber with access to the links land. Against the magnificent backdrop of the Mountains of Mourne and the golden sands of Dundrum Bay, the course first took shape under the hand of Old Tom Morris, who, as legend would have it, was enticed from Scotland for the princely sum of four guineas to identify locations for tees and greens within the natural corridors of the site's wild sand hills and gorse. The club's longstanding captain, George Combe, reworked Morris' original design over the next several years and then invited Harry Vardon to make further suggestions on visits to the links in 1908 and 1919. Finally, in 1920, Harry S. Colt added a few finishing touches.

Royal County Down's designer pedigree of Morris, Vardon and Colt complemented each other and the land which they were asked to work. For this threesome shared a fundamental principle on course design, namely, to reveal the course within the natural contours and conditions of the land. What they achieved, and the club has since preserved, is a Victorian Age masterwork as subtle in its evidence of human hand and as grand and noble as St Andrews, lacking only a list of major professional championships in its history. With extraordinary views of heather-strewn hills, distant mountains, and village steeples from its many high teeing grounds, it affords, wrote the great golf writer, Bernard Darwin, *'the kind of golf that people play only in their dreams'*. A recent book of the same name called Royal County Down *'the links of heaven'*. [5]

There is no more wonderful spot to behold the wind-tossed terrain of the course and the postcard views beyond it than the tee on number nine. Described by Vardon as a hole that will 'exhilarate and terrify,' the ninth offers one of Royal County Down's typical blind drives (a blind shot, the Irish will point out, is only blind once) from an elevated tee across a broad expanse of knee-high fescue, exposed rock, and heather. The target is a marker post set in a ridge of high sand hills about 175 yards from the championship tees. The drive that carries this crest is rewarded twice – the stirring sight of the ball rising against the distant dark mass of Slieve Donard, and the view that awaits on the far side of the ridge. For stretching out nearly 60 feet below the hill's summit is a rectangular fairway carpet of perfect green that seems to disappear into a nineteenth-century landscape painting celebrating the harmony of man and nature. All of the elements are here – a dramatic mist-shrouded mountaintop, its flanks and valleys flowing to the sea in deep greens and purples, its shadows embracing a village of white walls and clay red rooftops. The faint hint of burning peat carried on the breeze from the town mingles with the sea air and further seals the scene in the senses of the beholder. **As the locals say,** the view is 'perpetual gazingstock'.

The approach to the green is no less spectacular. Bounded by the broken parallel lines of ever pinching sand hills,

#9, Royal County Down Golf Club

the fairway abruptly ends at two formidable sentry bunkers set in a low ridge about 40 yards short of the plateau green. Except for a sweep of closely cut rough that flows down the left slope of the green towards the first tee, the setting has a peculiar amphitheatre effect, not unlike the eighteenth at St Andrews, which finishes amidst the shadows of the town at the intersection of Golf Place and Links Road. At the Old Course, though, the arrival at this juncture marks the end of a round. At Royal County Down, it signals that another nine is still to be played on this marvellous course, which Herbert Warren Wind, the dean of American golf writers, celebrated as 'the sternest examination in golf I had ever taken'.

About a hundred miles south of Newcastle, along the same coast but across the now less troubled border of the two Irelands, is a layout which the great British amateur champion, Harold Hinton, described in 1902 as 'the most

#15, Portmarnock Golf Club, County Dublin

natural links in the world'. This is the Portmarnock Golf Club and it is as close to being a national treasure as any sporting grounds. Founded in 1894, the links occupy a wild and shaggy site on the southern half of a narrow peninsula jutting out into Dublin Bay. Golf had been played there for at least a decade or more on a short course privately owned by John Jameson, the Irish whiskey magnate. But, like the Old Course's vague origins, there is evidence to suggest that objects were sent flying across this inviting landscape even before then.

On Christmas Eve, 1893, though, William Pickeman, a golf-mad Scot living in Dublin who admired the site from a distance, rowed over from Sutton Peninsula with his friend, George Ross, and confirmed his sense of the land's potential for a worthy eighteen. With Jameson's approval, they invited Mungo Park from Scotland to serve as the club's first professional and to advise on the routing of the course. A year later on St Stephen's Day, with Jameson installed as the club's first secretary and a shack-like 'clubhouse' erected, Captain Ross launched a gutty with his hickory shafted driver down the first fairway along the estuary and club play began.

Over the years, a new clubhouse has been built to replace the original, which burned down in 1905, some holes were lengthened, and bunkers were added by the membership. But the course has remained remarkably true to its *fin de siècle* design, most notably its two looping nines with no two consecutive holes playing in exactly the same direction. In large measure, Portmarnock has preserved its original integrity because it lacks contrivance and complexity and those (including Harry Colt, Henry Cairnes, Eddie Hackett, and Fred Hawtree) who had been invited from time to time to suggest improvements largely left well enough alone. The result is a straightforward challenge that takes full advantage of the subtle contours of the land, punishing rough, and exposure to the elements, especially the fierce winds off the Irish Sea, to protect itself.

Unlike Royal County Down and Ballybunion, Portmarnock has few blind shots and no mountainous dunes, but its slick greens, bewildering array of bunkers, and length (7,136 yards) provide formidable defences against par. Reflecting on these matters, Harry Bradshaw, the legendary Irish pro who teamed with Christy O'Connor to win the Canada (now World) Cup in 1958, said that the course 'may be daunting … but there is more satisfaction to be gained from a moderate score around Portmarnock than a very low return elsewhere'. Portmarnock's enduring quality and challenge have attracted more major professional and amateur tournaments to its grounds than any course in Ireland and this has added to its deserved reputation as one of the hardest and fairest competitive venues in the world. It upset many that Ireland's inaugural opportunity to host the Ryder Cup in 2006 was not contested over these links, so perfect for match play, rather than the upscale, tourist-oriented parkland course at the K Club.

Several holes define the character of Portmarnock – especially the two long finishing par fours on each nine – but perhaps none more elegantly than the scenic 192-yard fifteenth. Cited by the game's elite from Henry Cotton to Arnold Palmer to Ben Crenshaw as 'one of the greatest short holes on earth', it sits hard by Dublin Bay, separated from the beach and out of bounds by a ridge of shaggy marram-covered dunes. Although only 15 feet above the beach, its pulpit tee is one of the highest points on the course and affords commanding views of the entire peninsula and the sea, including two prominent rocky sentinels off shore, Ireland's Eye and Lambay Island. It also sits completely exposed to the wind which, depending upon its ferocity and direction, can require any club from a wedge to a wood to reach the green.

Accuracy is as much an issue as distance, for the narrow, convex-sloped putting surface is guarded by a necklace of sod wall pot bunkers and a deep recess aptly named the Valley of Sin, reminiscent of the similarly-named unhappy depression before the eighteenth green on the Old Course at St Andrews. There is no safe play on this hole. If par or better is the object, the ball must carry the green and come to rest on it. When the wind is strong from the sea, the only hope of hitting the green is to swing the shot in from over the beach. If, as a popular survey of Irish courses declares, **'Providence intended Portmarnock to be a golf course'**, **there is no better example of divine design – with a touch of satanic cunning – than this seaside gem.** [6]

On Ireland's western shore, 'where the air is so soft that it smudges the words', [7] just below the meeting of the Shannon River and the Atlantic Ocean, rests a stretch of dune land that exhausts superlatives about its nature and destiny. Architects and players, poets and scribes have formed a brilliant chorus of praise for what exists there among the billowing sand hills and eerie valleys – Ballybunion.

Invited with Molly Gourlay to suggest improvements for the course in 1936, Tom Simpson said: 'The beauty of the terrain surpasses that of any course we know. Never for one moment did we imagine, or expect to find, such a really great course or such a glorious piece of golfing ground.'

#11, Ballybunion Golf Club, County Kerry

Herbert Warren Wind took up the beat in an article for *The New Yorker* in 1971: 'To put it simply, Ballybunion revealed itself to be nothing less that the finest seaside course I have ever seen.'

Among the pilgrims who wanted to see for themselves was Tom Watson, the five-time winner of The Open who knew something about links courses: 'After playing Ballybunion for the first time, a man would think that the game of golf originated here. There appears to be no man-made influence. It looks like a course laid out in land as it was back in the tenth century. In short, Ballybunion is a course on which many golf architects should live and play before they build a golf course.'

The quality of timelessness, which Watson recognised, particularly impressed the authors of *Links of Heaven:* 'It is not just the size or the wild look of the famous Ballybunion sand dunes, or the beauty of the seaside holes – it is the way the links fit so superbly into what nature has provided. Many golf courses are blessed with fine natural settings, but at Ballybunion one feels that the gods also designed the holes.'[8]

Even more so than either Royal County Down or Portmarnock, the origins of golf at Ballybunion are lost in speculation. Although the formation of the first club can be traced to 1891, it undoubtedly sprang from an already established interest in the game on this site. Moreover, it appears that the focus of play, whenever it commenced, was the stretch of dramatic oceanfront dunes, rather than the relatively flat grounds about 400 yards inland. In other words, the pioneers of the game at Ballybunion chose the hardest and most challenging terrain to send their featheries flying. One wonders if this was an act of contrition, especially considering the near location of their playing grounds to the town's cemetery, which now sits only a few haunting yards from the first tee.

The annals of the club mention Old Tom Morris, James Braid, and Jo McKenna, the latter who may also have had a hand in laying out Lahinch and Royal Dublin, as early influences on the course's original nine-hole design.

Whatever they contributed provided some guidance for Lionel Hewson, the longtime editor of the *Irish Golf* journal, who was formally commissioned to lay out the nine-hole stretch in 1906. Ballybunion remained this size until 1927, when the course added a second nine. This was the course that Tom Simpson reviewed, and which he concluded scarcely needed any improvement, as it prepared to host the Irish Amateur Open in 1937.

As surely as Alister MacKenzie, Donald Ross, Alec Campbell and other great golf architects attributed the brilliance of the Old Course at St Andrews to the absence of human meddling with its fundamental features, as anachronistic and quirky as some of them might be, so, too, Ballybunion commands those who have come to visit to look, but not touch. It is a course of spectacular beauty and no discernable weakness, offering eighteen distinctive holes that easily can be recalled after only one round. Ballybunion's memorability rests not only in the way its distinctive topography has embraced and formed the course, but also the shot value that accompanies its transit from the first drive to the last approach.

No hole more fully captures the elements of Ballybunion's greatness than the eleventh, a 454-yard masterpiece along the edge of the Atlantic. It is a hole that has earned the admiration of Tom Watson as one of the toughest in all of golf. It is an opinion fully shared by a growing number of Watson's fellow American pros – Tiger Woods, Mark O'Meara, David Duval, Phil Mickelson, and Mark Calcavecchia among them – who followed his lead in coming to Ballybunion to prep for The Open.

From an elevated tee bordering the cliffs above the rock-bounded beach to the right and some 70 feet below, players from the championship markers face a 200-yard carry through a channel of dunes, scrub brush, and deep rough to a narrow ribbon of tumbling fairway. In shallow, terraced parcels, the fairway meanders to a steep drop about 50 yards short of the raised green. No matter how long the drive, the shot to the green has to penetrate through two massive sand hills that stand like the Pillars of Hercules before the deep, undulating green. Unlike all but three other holes on the course, no sand bunkers guard this green. But none are needed to make it any more

#11, Ballybunion Golf Club, County Kerry

difficult. For set on the edge of the cliffs, it affords no room to the right, in which direction the green slopes, and offers gnarly, matted rough everywhere else. **'Such a combination of majesty and ferocity, of originality together with the integrity of the truly natural,'** wrote Jim Finegan, **'is rare indeed.'** [9]

Finegan's description of the eleventh at Ballybunion is a tribute to the entire course. It applies just as surely to Royal County Down and Portmarnock. For, though located on opposite coasts and different grounds, they share characteristics with Ballybunion that reflect the unique properties of the larger Irish landscape. Foremost among these is a sense of wildness, spaciousness, and spiritual presence.

Facing the vastness of the Atlantic Ocean, Ireland is Europe's westernmost outpost. Until the European discovery of the Americas, its location made it the remotest spot of the 'civilised' world. Its defining golf courses, especially these three, are echoes of the island's isolation, hoary with history. They sit among turbulent sand hills, border on broad, desolate beaches, struggle against tormenting winds and angry seas, and host a game that is essentially focused on a lonely, passionate pursuit – the efforts of a solitary individual to muster wit and skill for the challenges of the elements and the grounds.

To succeed at such a game, and in such an environment, has led many a player to invoke heavenly assistance – or entertain a Faustian bargain. It has connected many others, though, to the origins of the game itself – to a time before swing gurus, the Golf Channel, and the tortuous hooks, weights, straps, and braces that the Marquis de Sade golf laboratories have invented as instructional aides. The severe, elemental nature of these courses invites spiritual connection with some distant ancestor of the game who could not resist propelling an object over these beckoning landscapes. Golfers should no more come to Ireland to skip these links or to criticise their difficulty than to miss Dublin or complain that their Guinness is too warm.

Other spirits abide in these timeless grounds, too. The ghost of Old Tom Morris has been reported wandering the fairways and haunting the rough of Royal County Down. The Vision of Killasheen, a banshee-like creature, can be glimpsed – at the risk of shortening one's life – walking an ethereal bridge that leads from Ballybunion into the sea. The Grey Man, the fairy form of the ancient Celtic storm god, *an fear liath*, exerts his sinister influence through the thick fog that often shrouds these coastal courses. The sheerie can appear anywhere and the ill effects of their encounter – temporary derangement and aimless wandering over the countryside – suggest their particular attention to golfers.

Yes, there are memories in these landscapes and spirits in their mists. They are deeper than what has been recorded in the histories of these clubs and beyond what the eyes can see. Most importantly, they await both resurrection and reverie, the delightful consequence of giving oneself to the game and the land, not just trying to add more notches to one's golfing belt.

CHAPTER THREE

Myth, History and a Sense of Place

Those who the gods seek to destroy first, *learn how to play golf.*

Leslie Nielsen, *Bad Golf My Way* (1992)

I am the Wind that blows over the Sea,

I am the Wave of the Ocean,

I am the Roar of the Sea,

I am a Ray of the Sun,

I am the Fairest of Plants,

I am a Lake in the Plain,

I am the Craft of the Artificer,

I am the Spear-point that gives Battle,

I am the God that creates in the head of man the Fire of Thought.

Amhairghin, Milesian warrior/poet and Ireland's first druid (c. 700 BC)

That the origins of golf on the sites of Ireland's most renowned courses – Royal County Down, Portmarnock, and Ballybunion – are somewhat obscure is no fault of the game's historians. Rather, it is a commentary on the nature of history itself in Ireland and the general sense that nothing is quite what it seems in this land. **For the merger of actual events with spiritual experience and superstition has influenced a holistic sense of the past that often makes no distinction between what is remembered and what is imagined.**

Éire, the Irish-language name for the country, underscores this ambiguity. According to the *Lebor Gabala*, *(The Book of Invasions)*, a twelfth-century manuscript that traced the lineage of Ireland's great families to Adam, Éire was the wife of Mac Greine, a grandson of Dagda, the chief god of the Tuatha De Danann. This *tuath*, or tribe, literally translates as 'the people of the [mother] goddess Danu.' In short, this was the first family of Irish gods.

Although Éire is a worthy goddess for a land to honour with her name, the *Lebor Gabala* is pseudo-history at its most inventive. For not only did the monks and scholars who wrote it synchronise Irish history, they also synthesised it, forever entwining the gods and mortals of the land of Éire. Gods became mortal and mortals resembled gods.

The story of the Tuatha De Danann reveals these shifting roles and identities most clearly and importantly. For as the principal gods of the Irish Celtic pantheon, their place in the indigenous belief structure was so strong that they were not directly refuted by the early Christian missionaries and teachers. Instead, they were accommodated. For rather than acknowledge their existence as true gods and risk the worship of false idols, the monastic scribes incorporated their tales into the larger historical narrative of Ireland. Gods became mortal.

In this narrative, most fully revealed in the *Lebor Gabala*, the Tuatha De Danann arrived in Ireland from the Greek

Rock wall between holes #2 and #4, Tralee Golf Club, Country Kerry

isles towards the end of a series of invasions that are traced to survivors of the great Flood of the Old Testament. Their magic and power, however, were unable to resist the Milesians, a warrior tribe supposedly from Spain, who landed in a large fleet at Kenmare Bay on the southwest coast around 700 BC. In other words, they reached Ireland shortly before the Celts, thus leading the medieval chronicles to anoint the Sons of Mil as the immediate ancestors of the Celts.

In two epic battles fought in the high mountains of Slieve Mish in Kerry and Taillten in Meath, the Milesians defeated the Tuatha De Danann. The power of their magic and arts was such, though, that the Tuatha De Danann escaped enslavement and annihilation. Rather, they were banished to a new kingdom of their creation beneath the earth and its waters and upon the distant islands of the sea. Among the land sites where the gods supposedly dwell and provide inspiration are two peaks in County Kerry, just southeast of Killarney, called the Paps of Danu. They are astonishingly shaped like the breasts of a woman, complete with 'nipples' that top their 700-metre heights. It is in such places of 'mother earth' where the gods are believed to reside and whence they occasionally emerge from their caves and sacred mounds in the form of 'the little people' – fairies and leprechauns and other such spirits – to pester and delight the surface dwellers.

The sense of divine and ancestral spirits within the land and upon it, thus firmly formed in myth, folk voice, and history, affects all aspects of Irish life and culture and conversation. Recognising this helps us understand that a caddie's explanation for a lost ball – 'The gods have it' – is not merely a colourful expression for the entertainment of his player or a great excuse. After all, who could possibly dispute divine will? It is, quite simply, the way it is, especially at a course like Tralee within view of the Slieve Mish mountains and the influence of the ancient spirits who dwell there.

No golf course in Ireland more fully connects to the history and mythology of the country than the Waterville Golf Links. Located at the far end of the Ring of Kerry, upon the sand hills and strand bordering Ballinskelligs Bay on Ireland's rugged southwest coast, Waterville witnessed golfing activity as early as the 1870s. The pioneers of the game in this remote land were the workers who manned a transatlantic cable station relaying messages between Europe and North America.

The grounds over which they played hardly constituted a defined course. It was not much more than tumbling meadowland, but it offered the kind of sandy links terrain that was irresistible for the ball strikers among the cable men. Relying on sheep to mow pathways, and the natural mounds and hollows to suggest tees and greens, the nineteenth-century golfers at Waterville experienced the game in its most primordial state. Even when some modest design attention was brought to the course around the turn of the century, its promise was more rumoured than delivered, especially regarding the unexplored dunes along the coast. Still, the playing quality and beauty of the nine-hole layout drew appreciative reviews. An article in the 1897 *Sportsman's Holiday Guide*, for example, declared that 'The green is considered a sporting one, and the views from it are very fine while the Atlantic breezes that blow across it are invigorating and refreshing.'

Contributing to the creation of Ireland's golfing heritage was a fitting role for Waterville to play, for the region had already provided a key element in the country's larger creation myth. This focused on the legendary arrival in Ballinskelligs Bay of Cesair and her brother, Ladra, two of the grandchildren of Noah who were sent to Ireland to escape the great Flood of the Old Testament. The landing near Waterville was among several which they and their companions – 50 other women and two other men – made along the southwestern and southern coasts. At each stop, one of the men and a third of the women disembarked with the explicit purpose of populating the land. Ladra took his cohort ashore at Waterford Harbor and apparently undertook his assignment with great enthusiasm. Unfortunately, it proved too much for him and he died heroically, according to the *Lebor Gabala*, from 'excess of women'.

Ladra had died, it would seem, from exhaustion, not dysfunction, as he and his other male shipmates, Bith and Fintan, fathered a huge progeny. Their descendants spread not only throughout Ireland, but also to the European continent and as far away as Asia Minor. Bith, for example, took his seventeen maidens to the north of Ireland, where he eventually succumbed to his carnal labors and old age and was buried on the Ulster mountain named after him, Slieve Beagh. The subsequent wanderings of the offspring of Ireland's first 'invaders' provided the Irish with the 'evidence' to claim that they were responsible for the rebirth of human civilisation after the Deluge. Indeed, in the mythic constructions of some Asian and European countries, Cesair and her women companions are regarded as their own ancestresses and goddesses.

Just as Waterville witnessed one of the landings of Ireland's first invaders, so, too, did it accommodate the country's last before the Celts. As already noted, these were the Milesians, led by Eber Dunn, the eldest of the Sons of Mil. According to the ancient annals, the patriarch of this family was a Scythian mercenary soldier who had served several clients, including the Pharaoh Nectanebus. Although small in number, the Milesians overcame the Tuatha De Danann in battle and influenced the shape of Ireland's warrior aristocracy for centuries to come. Many of the archaeological sites uncovered on the Iveragh Peninsula surrounding Waterville, like Staigue Fort, are attributed to the Milesians.

As if the mythological invaders and fertile settlers of Ireland were not enough to provide a rich, spiritual aura for Waterville, more formally recorded history added another layer. The religious and cultural conflicts in Ireland between Catholics and Protestants, the Gaelic Irish and royalist English, reached a savage climax with the outbreak of civil war in England in 1642 between the Parliamentary forces led by Oliver Cromwell and the loyalists of Charles I. Taking advantage of the confused situation in England, Irish Catholics arose in open rebellion against the Crown's authority and supporters, most notably the Protestant lords who had received generous land grants throughout Ireland for their loyalty. The rebellion quickly turned ugly and violent. In Ulster, the Catholic rebels drove many Protestants from their homes and killed many others. Rumours swirled about the extent of the carnage creating a belief in England that tens of thousands of Protestant loyalists had perished. The stage was set for vengeance.

Cromwell himself enacted it. Landing an army of 20,000 men in Ireland in September 1649, he laid siege to the Catholic garrison at Drogheda near the mouth of the River Boyne. When the garrison refused to surrender, Cromwell ordered all within to be put to death as a warning to other towns. For the next nine months, Cromwell's army raged throughout the country, enacting a similar massacre at the port town of Wexford on the southeastern coast, and terrorising the Catholic population everywhere. Catholic priests were outlawed, and those who remained in Ireland risked hanging or deportation to the West Indies, where hundreds of Catholics had been sold into slavery. Many more Catholic proprietors were stripped of their land holdings and possessions and driven

#12, Waterville Golf Links, County Kerry

like cattle to the poor province of Connacht, west of the Shannon River.

Waterville and the southwest did not escape the terror of the Penal Days unleashed by the Lord Lieutenant and General of the Parliament. Facing the ban on their religion, yet committed to its practice, Catholics throughout the region found ways to hide their priests and celebrate Mass in secret. Those in the coastal villages, like Waterville, often trekked out to remote spots along the coastline and concealed themselves from Cromwell's spies within the dunes to receive the sacraments. The deep depression below the green on the twelfth hole at Waterville, the 'Mass Hole', was a frequently used site for these secret services.

Today, the twelfth still inspires a prayer or two. From the championship tee set high upon an exposed dune, it is a brilliant three par of 200 yards over the blessed chasm to a fairly generous green. Although no bunkers guard the green, it is hardly defenseless. Any tee shot not carrying the putting surface will careen backwards into the holy hollow. Any ball hit beyond the green will be confounded by the tall grass and steep upslope awaiting there.

The twelfth is one of Eddie Hackett's favourite par threes in all of Ireland. One of the most influential figures in the history of Irish golf architecture, Hackett had been invited by the wealthy, Irish-born American, Jack Mulcahy, in 1970 to rescue the original nine holes from their near derelict condition, the consequence of years of neglect. Although Mulcahy came to Waterville primarily for its trout and salmon fishing, he was also an avid golfer, a member of New York's Winged Foot Golf Club. He recognised the potential for an extraordinary links through integrating the flats and dunes bordering the Inny estuary. So Mulcahy purchased the land, hauled Winged Foot's head professional, former Master's champion Claude Harmon, over to inspect it, and hired Hackett to design it. **Or, rather, as the Irish architect preferred,** *'to find it'*.

After walking the grounds for several days before declaring what he thought of its prospects, Hackett explained that he was looking for 'inspiration as to where to start it, how it would flow'. Whether the goddess Cesair or the gods of the Milesians or the spirits of the defiant Catholics provided it, we'll never know. But Hackett found what he was looking for and, helped considerably by Mulcahy's ready chequebook, he delivered a masterpiece – a 'magnificent monster' as Sam Snead characterised the 'new' Waterville Golf Links shortly after its opening in 1973.

The course drew enthusiastic reviews immediately. Raymond Floyd named Waterville among his five favourite courses in the world, in the same lofty company as Augusta National, Cypress Point, Pebble Beach, and the Old Course at St Andrews. The holder of four Grand Slam titles, Floyd said Waterville 'is one of the most beautiful places I have ever seen ... some of the finest links I have ever played'. Tom Watson thought that the set of par threes there might be the best in the world. Three-time British Open

#9, Waterville Golf Club, County Kerry

champion, Henry Cotton, proclaimed Waterville to be 'one of the greatest courses ever built. If it were located in Britain', he declared, 'it would undoubtedly be a venue for the Open Championship. **I have never seen such a consistent succession of really strong and beautiful holes than I have seen here.'** Such reviews continue to define Waterville and the course has consistently been ranked among the top 50 international courses by *Golf Digest*, while several of its holes have been celebrated among the best in the world.

Among the holes which have secured Waterville's reputation is the eleventh, perhaps the most natural links hole on the course, and about which Gary Player said is *'the most beautiful and satisfying par five of them all'*. It offers a twisting, tumbling journey of 500 yards through an alternately pinching and broadening valley of

#11, Waterville Golf Club, County Kerry

gorse-covered sand hills to a bunkerless green perched on a tiny mesa. Aptly named 'Tranquility', it is so secluded from the rest of the course that it feels like a private sanctum. Indeed, it likely served as a pathway for those persecuted Catholics of the seventeenth century who took this route to the Mass dell of the next hole. Today, when the late day shadows are just right, the channelled fairway of the eleventh recalls those spiritual treks for **'it feels about as close to heaven as golf gets'.** [1]

There is much more to praise at Waterville. The back nine, especially, may be unsurpassed among links courses for variety, challenge, and balance. It stretches a hefty 3690 yards from the back tees, each hole routed brilliantly through the dunes and all shots affected by the unrelenting Atlantic winds. The inward nine presents a succession of memorable holes and scenes that culminates at Mulcahy's Peak, a mid-length par three over an unforgiving wasteland of thick gorse and grass, and a majestic five par finishing hole bordered its entire 582 yards by Ballinskelligs Bay to the right.

The closing holes afford two further encounters with the spirits that abide at Waterville. The tee on seventeen rests on the flattened summit of the highest dune on the course. It was from this inspiring spot overlooking the entire rumpled and rolling landscape of the links that Mulcahy and Hackett plotted elements of Waterville's design together. With the sea to the right and the muscular Macgillycuddy's Reeks, containing Ireland's highest mountain, Carrauntoohil, flexing through the low clouds on the eastern horizon, it is the kind of place where one contemplates eternity. Jack Mulcahy apparently thought so, too, because an urn containing his ashes is buried beneath the championship tee box. Bowing to place a tee in the ground here is somewhat an act of homage to Mulcahy, his love of the game, and the vision that inspired Waterville.

Another Waterville spirit overlooks the ninth and eighteenth greens, welcoming players as they complete their nines. For here stands a life-size statue of Payne Stewart, the two-time US Open champion, who died tragically in a bizarre plane crash in October 1999. Like so many of the game's greatest players, including Tiger Woods, Mark O'Meara, David Duval, and Ernie Els, who have tasted Waterville's charms and challenges, Stewart had come to Waterville as a tune-up for the British Open.

Stewart's affection for the place, though, went beyond the links. It embraced the town, its citizens, and, like Mulcahy, the immense natural beauty of the area. In September 1999, on the occasion of the Ryder Cup matches at Brookline, Massachusetts, Waterville demonstrated its appreciation of Stewart's friendship and bestowed on him the Honorary Captaincy of the Club. It was the last golf honour he would receive before his death. Now his likeness, like his once flowing swing, graces both the memory of the game and the grounds of *these mystical links in the land of Éire where the gods of myth and faith and whimsy co-mingle and consort.*

Statue of Payne Stewart, overlooking the ninth green,
Waterville Golf Links, County Kerry

THE RAIN HERE IS ABSOLUTE, MAGNIFICENT, AND FRIGHTENING. To call this rain bad weather is as inappropriate as to call scorching sunshine fine weather. You can call this rain bad weather, but it is not. It is simply weather, and weather means rough weather. It reminds us forcibly that its element is water, falling water. *And water is hard.*

Heinrich Boll, *Irish Journal* (1983)

CHAPTER FOUR

The Broom of Nature

Storm flag, The Island Club, County Dublin

Wind and rain are great challenges. *They separate the real golfers.*

Let the seas pound against the shore, let the rain pour.

Tom Watson, Winner of 8 Majors including 5 British Opens

'Once more the storm is howling, and half hid

Under this cradle-hood and coverlid

My child sleeps on. There is no obstacle

But Gregory's wood and one bare hill

Whereby the haystack – and roof-leveling wind,

Bred on the Atlantic, can be stayed.'

William Butler Yeats, 'A Prayer For My Daughter' (1919)

84

They are called squibs, brief showers which can occur anytime, anywhere, along the Irish coast. They emanate from seemingly clear skies as easily as overcast ones, and no matter their origin, rarely last for more than a few minutes. They also arrive in different degrees of intensity depending upon the winds that accompany them.

Sometimes the first drops arrive almost apologetically. Large and scattered, they afford a false sense that their falling can be gauged and dodged. Within seconds of the initial sprinkles, though, a torrent of water that might even have given Noah pause can pound upon the uninitiated victims of Irish weather. Caught completely in the open, players will huddle pathetically under their umbrellas and marvel at the ferocity and effect of the deluge. A field of vision may be reduced to no more than a few yards, although a tantalising brightness can glow beyond the curtain of falling water. Huge puddles instantly appear in the fairway, each glistening like melting silver, the rain drops kicking up frenzied splashes like crowds of leprechauns exulting at a rock concert. **The rain comes down straight, hard, heavy, and loud.** *And then it is gone.* Not even a gentle tapering or a whispered retreat. *It just stops.*

But squibs are as ornery as their alleged celestial authors. They particularly will treat with contempt those whose ignorance of their nature or presumption of their passing relaxes their guard. As the alliance of wind and rain strengthens, the consequences become more fearful. White caps appear in the shallowest of streams. Routes to rain shelters achieve greater importance. Golf swings dissolve like the witch Elphaba in the shock of Dorothy's water.

Serious weather is not an anomaly in Ireland. Most say it is the consequence of location and geology that have created a unique set of climatic and golfing conditions. The Emerald Isle is, first and foremost, an island, a relatively small one at that, covering about 36,000 square miles. But, although the country stretches 300 miles at its longest and nearly 200 at its widest, there is no place in Ireland that is more than 70 miles from some stretch of coastline.

The surrounding waters have two significant influences on the country. First, the tighter range of temperature variations at sea than on land effect a more temperate climate overall with less extremes. Daytime temperatures in the summer hover mostly in the mid-60s (°F) with a night-time drop-off of rarely more than a dozen degrees. Although freezing conditions, including snow, can occur in some northern and eastern regions during the winter months, Ireland affords play year round, at least for the hearty.

Second, the Gulf Stream, a powerful current of warm surface water flowing from the Caribbean northward across the Atlantic, passes very close to the Irish coastline west and south. Accompanying the Gulf Stream are the prevailing southwesterly winds that bring the moisture-laden warm air ashore and provide an additional ameliorating influence on Ireland's climate. Each of these conditions contributes to the vast greenness of the land and such startling sights as palm trees and other subtropical vegetation in parts of the lush southwest.

This is the good news. The evil twin of all this movement of air and ocean is that the activity can be intense, fast moving, and unpredictable. Huge depressions regularly form in the Atlantic as the southwesterly winds collide with the much cooler air descending from the northern latitudes. Since Ireland is the first landmass that these depressions encounter as they move west to east, Europe's last outpost is the weather's first target. The western counties, Sligo, Mayo, Galway, Clare, and Kerry, bear the brunt of this assault of wind and water on Ireland's coast. Their experience with these conditions has influenced a virtual sub-genre of Irish literature, including the writings of Sean O'Faolain, Louis MacNeice, Benedict Kiely, Stephen Rynne, and Robert Lloyd Praeger.[1]

There are others, though, who attribute the sweeping rains and shouting seas to sources that defy scientific explanation. For long before writers discovered the moorlands and cliffs, mountains and coasts of this 'most lonesome region',[2] the gods of the Celts and their predecessors gathered and raged in the west, the critical region of the Irish foundation myth. Aligned with one tribe or another, they emerged from sea and sky like 'the high keen of a lost Lear-spirit in agony condemned for eternity to wander cliff and cove without comfort'.[3] Bearing such names as Manannan mac Lir, Gaeth, Balor, and Goll, these are spirits who do not exactly conjure up friendly images of still waters and gentle breezes. **Rather, these are gods with an agenda, foremost of which are distressing humans and exciting their imaginations.**

The earliest works of Irish literature chronicled the storms of weather and war brought by the gods. Most importantly, the *Lebor Gabala* recorded the victories of the Tuatha De Danaan over several pre-Milesian invaders. The Fir Bolgs of Connacht, for example, fell to Danu's champions at the first battle of Moytura, near the Galway-Mayo border village of Cong on Lough Corrib. It is there that John Ford in 1951 fashioned his own myths about Ireland when he directed John Wayne and Maureen O'Hara in *The Quiet Man*, an idealised Hollywood portrait of

Atlantic storm clouds, County Clare

mid-twentieth-century Irish life. After their defeat, the Fir Bolgs fled to the Aran Islands in Galway Bay, where the islands' gruesome weather and bleak stone forts are attributed to them. The most spectacular of the latter is Dún Aonghasa, whose elaborate defences and semi-circular terraced walls cover over 400 cliffside acres above the furious surf of Inishmore.

An even fiercer foe, the Fomorians, a one-armed, one-legged race of swarthy giants, according to the ancient chronicles, arrived in ships from Scandinavia, established a base on Tory Island, beyond the north-west tip of County Donegal, and launched raids along the western coast. But they, too, fell to the martial arts and magic of the preternaturally skilled De Danaan under the command of Lugh Lamfhota, the Irish god of sun and light. The decisive battle took place on a plain near Sligo, north of Lough Arrow, and forever secured a high place for Lugh in the pantheon of the Irish Heroic Age.

Just as Lugh was the favourite god of his Age, his son, Cúchulainn, was the most beloved 'mortal'. His deeds are recorded in a series of tales known as The Ulster Cycle, which includes the greatest work of classical Irish literature, the *Tain Bo Cuailgne (The Cattle Raid of Cooley)*. First committed to writing in the seventh century, the *Tain* evolved over centuries. The story that it tells – 'some true, some not, some for the delight of fools' – is the culmination of a long battle that stormed across the north of Ireland between the realms of Connacht and Ulster.[4]

If the *Tain* is the Irish *Iliad*, then Cúchulainn is the Irish Achilles. Unsurpassed in courage, honour, and physical beauty, Cúchulainn is the ideal warrior-aristocrat. Capable of whipping himself into a monstrously distorted 'warp spasm', a virtually indestructible heroic rage, the great champion had no fear and no equal – and no humility. Only the use of magic by the Connacht goddess-queen, Meadhbh, stilled his sword. His death after single-handedly battling Meadhbh's forces for weeks, including slaying 130 enemy kings, is a model of heroic sacrifice that Irish Nationalists would invoke in the nineteenth and twentieth centuries.

The northwestern Irish landscape over which much of this bloody 'history' played out is as harsh and unforgiving as the tales and the heroes themselves. Hosting the fiercest winds and the heaviest rains that visit the country, it is a region where, even in sunlight, the 'land looks damp'.[5] The meeting of sea and land on this bold and rugged coast is no more spectacularly realised than the Cliffs of Moher, a 5-mile stretch of terrifying high rock in County Clare standing in defiant opposition to the Atlantic. Few trees appear along the coast and those that do survive are bent in grotesque homage to the power of the winds. Similarly, the salt-laden winds and the constant pounding of the sea against the coastland have a murderous effect on other plant life. There are relatively few calm days anywhere on the western coast, but, somewhat reassuringly, there are even fewer Force 10 gales with winds in excess of 55 miles per hour as well. The latter, though, just seem to be blowing when it's time to take the first tee.

Like many of the world's greatest courses – Augusta National, Merion, and Cypress Point in the United States, for example, and Muirfield, Carnoustie, and Turnberry in Scotland – the first hole on many of Ireland's finest courses introduces players to the character of the course, not necessarily its teeth. Although none possess the antiquarian quirkiness of Prestwick with its railway tracks immediately adjacent to the first tee, or the intimidation of the Old Course at St Andrews where one can imagine the disapproving faces of several centuries of Royal and Ancient membership peering through the high windows of the clubhouse behind the tee, the start of an Irish round has both familiar and unique dimensions. **Weather and place mark both.**

The Irish weather, ranging from the gentle mists of 'soft days' to furious conditions that redefine the concept of par, is part of the shared experience of golf in Ireland. It makes its distinctive contribution to other commonly felt joys and satisfactions of the game, especially the elements of surprise and anticipation.

The former has as much to do with unexpectedness as wonder. Although there is a passive aspect to surprise, as when one is taken completely unawares by a roiling squib out of the blue, there is also an active element. The latter involves a willingness to be surprised, to risk, in fact, activities and circumstances that are somewhat uncertain and unpredictable. And we are all capable of daring because all serious daring comes from within. Chance plays as important a role in golf as the physical skills and the problem-solving abilities that it demands. To bring daring to this game – a demanding course ventured, a difficult shot attempted, a blustery day engaged – acknowledges its nature and invites surprise. Wonder accompanies a game that not only reveals so much about those who play it, but also offers so many marvellous possibilities in the consequences of its pursuit.

Similarly, anticipation has two meanings, one more active than the other. First, there is the sense of hopeful expectation that accompanies something that one looks forward to doing. In a land where weather is rarely, if ever, an excuse for cancelling a golf game, understanding that you will get wet from the rain and walloped by the wind is the first step in accepting what the round may provide. The same is true for the grounds over which the game will be played. For knowing the important characteristics of links land golf before the round begins will increase the enjoyment of the experience. The strokes that such knowledge might save are an extra bonus. Golf, or anything, for that matter, is unlikely enjoyed if approached with dread or as a form of penance. 'Suffering,' says Fred Shoe-maker, a California teaching professional who incorporates elements of Zen in his approach, 'is not a prerequisite for golf.'[6]

Second, anticipation is rooted in experience. The images that one chooses to recall from experience provide a prescient foundation for what awaits. **This is the essence of envisioning a golf shot.** With a sense from prior experience of what a successful shot entails, one can anticipate, that is, foresee, what needs to be accomplished with the shot now at hand. Summoning such positive images will not always produce a brilliantly-executed, knockdown five iron draw stiff to the flagstick on number fifteen at Portmarnock, but there is a greater likelihood of pulling off something equally satisfying if one has a sense that such is possible. Hope is at the heart of this game, for it promises what might be.

The first tee brings all of these elements together and Ireland has its fair share of first tees that do not disappoint the expectations for a memorable experience that players bring to their rounds. Ranging from the grand sea panoramas of Tralee and County Wicklow, to the adjacent graveyards at Ballybunion and Portmarnock Links, to the castle hotel backdrops of Adare Manor and Dromoland, to the dunes sweep of the Island Club and Portstewart, the splendour of the views and variety of the grounds are eloquent testimony to how **golf, like no other, is a game as much shaped by the land as joined to it.**

Weather strengthens the bond, as the famous Scottish saying, 'Nae wind, nae rain, nae golf,' affirms. Without the wind, golf 'would be like playing snooker'. [7] With the wind, but absent the unique characteristics of true links land courses, the game would be impossible. For unlike the target golf conditions of most American courses – soft, receptive greens, lush fairway grasses, and distinct cuts of fairway and gradations of rough – **the game is played much closer to the ground on Irish links, than above it.** Only a thin layer of topsoil covers the stretches of sand flats and dunes that exist between the beach and the main land mass, that, in fact, *link* them. But this soil supports extremely rugged grasses, such as fescue and bent, which are usually cut short on fairways and greens and ignored only a few yards, sometimes a few feet, beyond. The result is a lot of roll. Irons replace drivers off the tee. High wedge lobs quickly give way to putters from the fairway 40 yards off the green. And one's golfing vocabulary expands to the bump-and-run, the pitch-and-run, the knockdown, and, most assuredly, new adjectives for the penal rough and new, desperate commands for 'stop'.

No course in Ireland offers a more memorable or anticipated playing experience through connecting the elements of weather, first tee setting, timelessness, and golfing heritage than Lahinch. In these and other respects, as Herbert Warren Wind first pointed out, Lahinch is the 'St Andrews of Ireland'. A major difference, though, is that the old Scot's town on the North Sea offers an array of attractions besides its golfing grounds, while Lahinch is singularly devoted to the ancient game.

A band of Scots, in fact, brought the game to Lahinch in 1892. They were members of the Black Watch Regiment stationed in Limerick who had recognised the potential for establishing a wonderful links within the mountainous dune country lining the shore of Liscannor Bay. The man they asked to lay out the course, Old Tom Morris, agreed. For one pound and travel expenses, Morris completed the task quickly. For other than designating locations for tees and greens, he felt there was little else he needed to do. **'I consider the links as fine a natural course as it has ever been my good fortune to play over,'** he declared. His endorsement and a newly completed railway link to Dublin helped Lahinch become Ireland's foremost golfing destination by the turn of the century.

The little village on the west coast, about midway between Galway Bay and the River Shannon, was already a tourist mecca when the Lahinch Golf Club formally organised in 1893. Visitors came to see the Cliffs of Moher, visible from the golf course only 3 miles away, and to walk the Burren, an otherworldly landscape of gray and green limestone another few miles to the northeast. Resembling a giant rock garden, the Burren is home to a brilliant assemblage of plants and flowers, many uniquely co-existing in this strange site. Within its roughly 100 square miles of terrain, the Burren also contains a rich array of archaeological remains from Neolithic times to medieval. Hundreds of ring forts, dolmens, and grave and tomb sites share the area with the ruins of towers, churches, monasteries, and high crosses.

Several holy wells can also be found in or near the Burren, including St Brigid's Well in Liscannor, just north of Lahinch. The reputed healing powers of the well's waters have their roots in ancient Celtic belief and a cult surrounding Brigit, the alleged offspring of a union between a druid priestess and Dagda, the great god of the Tuatha De Danaan. As the merger of Irish history and mythology so often accomplishes, Brigid exists as both goddess and saint, the latter designation occurring when her namesake, Brigid of Kildare, was converted to Christianity by St Patrick in the fifth century. The second Brigid later became the high abyss of a monastery and a bishop. Revered for her kindness and respect for the old traditions, Ireland's 'second patron saint' fashioned a simple straw symbol, St Brigid's Cross, which is a common sight in many Irish homes. Its sun-wheel, four-armed design signifies the four seasons of the year and the unity of the country's Celtic and Christian cultures.

With its spectacular coastal setting, a magic well as a neighbour, the O'Brien Castle ruins on its property, and the blessings of Old Tom Morris, Lahinch possesses all of the elements of a great Irish links. It further strengthened its designer appeal when the club engaged Alister MacKenzie in 1927 to suggest improvements on both

Morris' work and that of Charles Gibson, the professional at Westward Ho!, who had made some changes in the original routing in 1907 in order to accommodate the greater distances achieved with the new rubber-cored Haskell ball. MacKenzie's principal contributions were to place all eighteen holes within the dunes and to leave untouched two of Morris' most whimsical touches, 'Klondyke' and 'Dell', now holes four and five. More recently, the course has undergone a significant make over under the supervision of Martin Hawtree aimed at restoring the MacKenzie characteristics that had been lost through alterations in the 1930s. The result of Hawtree's work is as grand a restoration as can be witnessed at any of the great manor houses or gardens throughout the country.

MacKenzie's decision, affirmed by the club's present membership, to leave 'Klondyke' and 'Dell' alone is a gift to the golfing world. For these holes with their blind shots, crossing fairways, and straddling dunes provide a window on another century when such design features were in vogue. To have altered them or taken them out of play would be as unthinkable as removing the railroad ties from the Cardinal Bunker at Prestwick or replacing the road behind the green on the seventeenth at the Old Course with a grassy swale. Instead, golfers can enjoy a journey back in time, as long as they bring with it a sense of humour.

'Klondyke' is almost sane. From an elevated tee, with their backs to the beach, players face a virtual box canyon – a narrow, isolated valley pinched by steep dunes on either side and a huge, fuzzy sand hill at its end, about 330 yards away. But the card says the hole is 472 yards. A warning notice near the base of the distant dune provides the answer to the question about what to do next:

Flagman signaling it is clear to hit over the crossing dune,
#4, Lahinch Golf Club, County Clare

SPECIAL WARNING re KLONDYKE: 4th Hole.

> **The Committee of Lahinch Golf Club wish to inform**
>
> **all players that they will not accept liability for accidents**
>
> **at the crossing of the 4th and 18th fairways.**
>
> **It is the responsibility of each individual golfer to ensure**
>
> **that there is no one on the crossing before he plays over Klondyke.**

Yes, *over* 'Klondyke'. During the high golfing season, the shot over the dune is assisted by a flagman who pops into view near the top of the ridge, like a target in a shooting gallery, ready to signal when the fairway beyond is clear. When he is not performing his signaling duties, he hides in a nasty-looking little wooden shelter that is stuck

#5, Lahinch Golf Club, County Clare

into the dune on the green side of the hole. From all appearances, both the flagman and his shelter could have been placed there by Old Tom.

The 'Dell' hole is an even greater enigma. If the second shot on 'Klondyke' is baffling, the tee shot on the par three sixth is pure theatre – Gilbert and Sullivan, that is. The target is a small, whitewashed stone placed near the top of a dune about 140 yards from the tee. An equally high dune sits behind this one. Of course, there is no clue that this is the case from the tee. Sandwiched between the two dunes is a narrow corridor, about 10 yards wide, upon which the green is placed. Again, there are no clear clues to this arrangement, except a caddie's instructions and a vague drawing in the course guide. Such are the way things are on the world's ultimate blind hole, a design so ancient it might be considered post-modern.

The object is to fly the stone, which is moved each day to reflect the placement of the flagstick, and then hope for the best. Either the fronting or backstop dune should yield a carom to the green, but not always. If not, one faces a nearly impossible chip from a severe downhill lie in high grass to a slick, narrow green. Such a situation is not likely to evoke kind thoughts about Old Tom Morris. But that is not the point of the hole. This is a museum piece and it seems perfectly at home among the other curiosities of Lahinch.

Those curiosities reveal themselves even before a round begins. An old barometer, long broken, hangs in the clubhouse. It still foretells the weather, although not in its long-frozen dial. Rather a small sign posted under it advises: 'See goats'. Yet, the sign itself is a mystery for its cryptic message refers to the club's former small herd of Burren goats which used to wander freely upon the course. When the weather was good (a relative term, to be sure), they roamed the dunes, often at the north end of the course in the grassy slopes above the tenth green and along the par three eleventh. When the weather was less suitable, at least, for goats, they retreated to the lee of the clubhouse next to the first tee. Alas, the goats no longer add their bleats to the general commotion around the first tee. For they were victims of the foot and mouth epidemic that swept Ireland and the United Kingdom in 2001, although members and caddies acknowledge that shooting the goats may have been 'a somewhat extreme' response to the disease. Their absence, though, hardly makes Lahinch's first tee a less intimidating stage from which to begin a round. Boxed on three sides by buildings, walkways, and a busy car park, it affords no place to hide and players are happy to launch anything respectable to commence their round.

Something more than respectable, though, is generally needed to start a round well at Lahinch and to sustain it. The opening hole is a stern uphill par four of 381 yards to a table-top green protected by bunkers and steep drop-offs that plays much longer than the posted length. Players face not only a formidable climb, but also the prevailing winds that sweep down to the crowded tee and then swirl around it. Yet, it is a fair introduction to the course, except 'Klondyke' and 'Dell', of course, for which no introduction is possible. The first and a brilliant stretch of holes from the sixth to the eleventh, which rival any at Ballybunion, Waterville, or Royal County Down, underscore the time-tested design qualities of the links and the brutal truth that its shot-making requirements will reveal all the flaws in one's game.

Rivalling the flagman's shelter on four and a fox's den on ten, which is burrowed in the face of a greenside bunker for protection from the elements, is a mineshaft-looking shed on the eighth hole. Officially, it is a rain bunker. But that requires considerable imagination. Little more than a few upright boards with a sheet of corrugated metal as a roof, it is pressed into a shaggy, cone-shaped dune. The high grass leading to and nearly engulfing it suggests that this structure has rarely been used. It is no wonder. Once surrounded by the devil-eyed Burren goats, and now, surely, their ghosts, it is situated on one of the remotest parts of the course. Some castle dungeons are more inviting than this place. It would not be surprising to find a Dante-inspired note attached to it some day warning those who might consider entering: 'Abandon all hope.'

Such are the sights and adventures that Lahinch affords. **'Savage as a tiger when the wind blows, mild and lovely on a sunny, calm day,'** described John Burke about his home course where he won many of his Irish amateur championships.[8] The great champion might well have been describing Ireland herself. Indeed, an anonymous Irish cleric, writing in the sixteenth century, marvelled how 'the broom of Nature'[9] swept all the elements of heaven and earth so sweetly and intensely across this land.

No matter what the weather, though, Lahinch occupies a unique and honoured place in the history of the game in Ireland. As Burke suggests, it demands everything from a Cúchulainn-like 'warp spasm' to the serenity of Brigit.

But what it offers in return are an unsurpassed golfing landscape and an unforgettable playing experience.

Time seems suspended on these links in a way that fully celebrates and reveals how the game is rooted in land and memory.

God, Almighty, first planted a garden and, indeed, it is the purest of human pleasures.

Francis Bacon, 'Of Gardens' (1625)

CHAPTER FIVE

Gardens of the Gods

When anyone sees Killarney,

even if he is the basest heretic,

he must believe in God.

Viscount Castlerosse, Earl of Kenmare (1939)

#12, Druids Glen Golf Club, County Wicklow

I think we may have honoured our brief to come up with Ireland's best inland course. Certainly we have tried, we have been given the freedom, the grand site, and the money to do the job.

Pat Ruddy, co-architect for Druids Glen (1996)

Flowers and pond near #12,
Druids Glen Golf Club, County Wicklow

Inland and upland from the fierce beauty of the links country, the pleasures of Irish golf also abound. Ringed by

an almost unbroken series of rugged coastal mountains, including the Macgillycuddy Reeks, the mountains of Mourne, Mweelrea, and Partry, and the Wicklow, Nephin Beg, and Antrim ranges, Ireland slopes like a giant bowl to a kinder interior of gentle hills and quilted fields. The lofty crags of the Achill peaks, Mount Brandon, and Carrauntoohil occasionally receive dustings of snow, which adds a ghostly quality to the bogs, meadows, and forests below. Within the deep blue and purple glens of the mountain shadows, ancient mill towns and villages sit upon the tributaries and passes of the land's many rivers, fed by the downward rush of so many brilliant streams. These waters help form Ireland's nearly 800 lakes, the largest of which, Lough Neagh, touches the shores of five of Northern Ireland's six counties.

The Irish interior was once a forest of spectacular density and fertility. Great stands of oak, elm, ash, alder, hazel, birch, and pine covered the countryside. Animals now long extinct in Ireland, such as the brown bear, wolf, and Irish Great Deer, whose magnificent antlers stretched over 10 feet, flourished beneath the primeval forest cover and on its border grasslands. The abundance of such unexploited flora and fauna made the land irresistible to humans, whose arrival some 10,000 years ago would eventually yield the Neolithic communities that depended upon arable farming and grazing. Pollen analysis and other dating techniques suggest that around 3500 BC an aggressive effort was underway to clear the land of trees in order to grow crops in the newly-opened fields and to graze stock on the newly-created pastures. Axes continued to fell the Irish forests for centuries, the final blows occurring in the seventeenth century when British proprietors in Ireland realised enormous profits from the sales of timber harvests in England, the Netherlands, and other European markets. Today, less than five per cent of the Irish landscape is forested and much of that is the result of recent reforestation and conservation efforts.

Several national forests and parks, most notably Killarney in County Kerry, Glenveagh in County Donegal, and the Wicklow Mountains National Park centred at Glendalough, provide a glimpse of Ireland's ancient landscape. There is golf here, too, and its play through valleys framed by thickly wooded slopes of conifer, cedar, juniper, and holly and along the edges of dark glacial lakes and rushing streams connects players to the memory of the land as surely as the essence of the game. This is not links land, but it is magnificent golfing country all the same.

For the game in such settings is no less immersed in Ireland's natural history, spirituality, and mythology than that played upon the seaside cliffs and shores.

The standard for all parkland courses in Ireland is the Killarney Golf and Fishing Club which, according to local tradition, traces play at its location along the northern banks of Lough Leane to 1891. All of the elements that underscore the most distinctive places in Irish golf – setting, history, particularity, and idiosyncrasy – form the story and character of this incomparable landscape, 'the end product of what the good Lord Almighty can do when He's in a good mood'.[1]

Dotting Killarney National Park's 25 square miles are enough castle ruins and abbeys, manor houses and cottages to employ the entire Irish calendar industry. But the three shimmering lakes within the park are the region's main attractions. Dozens of islands, most notably the largest, Innisfallen, where it is said that Brian Boru, the great Irish chieftain, and Brendan the Navigator were educated at St Fallen's monastery, sit within the lakes and the miles of pathways surrounding them. Almost all lead to a waterfall or stone bridge or other captivating spot to take in the splendid scenery. Tourists have been streaming to Killarney's lakes since the seventeenth century and many whom they have charmed, including Charlotte Brontë, Thomas Macauley, Sir Walter Scott, Alfred Lord Tennyson, William Thackeray, and Percy Bysshe Shelley, have not failed to sing the region's praises and promote its romantic image.

Golf at Killarney originated on a nine hole lay-out within Deer Park, part of the Earl of Kenmare's nearly 120,000-acre estate surrounding the town and the lakes. It was the good earl's son, Charles Valentine Browne, Viscount Castlerosse, however, who appreciated the possibilities of developing the old nine into something special, given the circumstances of its location and the expanding Irish tourism trade after the First World War. Establishing the Killarney Golf Club Ltd., Castlerosse engaged the British architect, Sir Guy Campbell, to help design a new eighteen-hole course on another piece of the Kenmare domain and enlisted his friend, Henry Longhurst, to publicise it. The Viscount's goal was for every visitor to 'return home, boosters to a man, and shout to all that they have never seen anything so fine as the Killarney Golf Course'.[2]

Somehow, Campbell resisted the more bizarre notions of his patron – such as colour-coordinating holes with the appropriate flora, equipping the entire course with a sound system to boom Beethoven's Ninth Symphony across it at noon each day, and planting trees in the middle of greens – and produced a design of lasting beauty and challenge. Despite his pre-Disneyland urges, Castlerosse did not lack talent as a designer. Several holes at Killarney – notably the short par five thirteenth on the Mahony's Point Course and the lakeside par three third and exquisite par four thirteenth holes on Killeen – reveal a keen sense for the fair and dramatic, qualities particularly enhanced by the views afforded of the Macgillycuddy Reeks and the ever-changing hues of Lough Leane. None of the glories of the setting were lost on Longhurst who dutifully proclaimed that **'Only a man devoid of soul could not rapture in the splendour and tranquility of Killarney Golf Club.'**

Perhaps Castlerosse's greatest contribution to golf in Ireland was his confidence that Killarney could be the premier inland destination for the game. He imagined a second course to complement the eighteen that opened in 1939, but died before his dream could be realised. Others, though, enacted that vision. Dr Billy O'Sullivan, a Killarney native who won the Irish Amateur in 1949, particularly championed expansion. Combining Castlerosse's ideas with those of Fred Hawtree, the pioneering Irish golf architect who directed significant design and routing changes on the original course in the late 1940s, O'Sullivan oversaw construction of the second eighteen.

It opened in 1972 to rave reviews, none more enthusiastically provided than by Fáilte Ireland, the Irish Tourist Board, which happily anticipated the economic benefits of 40,000-plus rounds a year. In 2001, overcoming years of opposition from several environmental groups, a third course, Lackabane, designed by Donald Steele and set in the woods on higher ground closer to the town, opened for play.

The main courses, Mahony's Point and Killeen, comprise a mixture of old and new holes, the latter especially focusing on a stretch along the lakeshore just west of the clubhouse. Eddie Hackett added some finishing touches in preparation for the Carrolls Irish Open contested over the Killeen Course in both 1991 and 1992, as did David Jones for the 1996 Curtis Cup. Contrary to what some feared, the two courses did not compromise the strength of the original Castlerosse/Hawtree/O'Sullivan eighteen. They are different, to be sure, with the nearly 300 yard longer Killeen affording a sterner test, yet Mahony's Point providing a greater glimpse of the Killarney golfing scene from an earlier era. On either course, though, players may find it hard to focus on the golf for the enchanting setting may be unsurpassed among inland courses anywhere. A lovely par three, the 170-yard tenth at Killeen, is aptly called 'Heaven's Own Reflex' by the locals. And standing on the tee, looking towards a perfectly oval green planted at the point of a peninsula and guarded by a small pond, beyond which arises Innisfallen Island out of the lake and Shehy Mountain above it, *it is hard to imagine a more beautiful place in the world.*

No less than the great links courses of Ireland, Killarney's two lakeside eighteens harmonise gracefully with their natural surroundings. The rhododendrons, azaleas, magnolias, and hydrangeas, of course, have been carefully planted, but they are neither shaped like fairies nor portrayed in plastic. Rather, a self-conscious reverence for nature characterises the scene. As most gardens borrow from the surrounding landscape for their greatest effects, the golf courses of Killarney do not aim to demonstrate human authority over nature. Rather, they celebrate their location through a design perspective that helps reveal the features of the lake country and the delights they provide for players who come here. If Killarney does not offer perfect happiness –

'Heaven's Own Reflex', #10, Killeen Course,
Killarney Golf and Fishing Club, County Kerry

golf, after all, is not a game of perfect – it does offer aesthetic pleasures that otherwise meet the requirements of Eden.

It is a divinely evocative place, and for good reason. No goddess was more important among the Celtic deities than Danu, the sun goddess and mother of the Irish gods, and no place more sacred to her than Munster, the province in which Killarney sits. For here she wielded her greatest power, manifested in the fertility and beauty of the land, as, for example, the Paps of Danu, and in the strength of her champions. The most important of these was the warrior-king Brian Boru, who successfully defended the southwest against Viking assaults in the late tenth century and briefly laid claim to the title of High King of all Ireland. In their serene beauty and powerful effect on Irish golf and tourism, Killarney's courses evince the blessings of Danu and the dominion of Brian. **They are places of pleasure and remembrance, a most appropriate destination for any golfing pilgrimage.**

Lake country of similar beauty and atmosphere hosts another of Ireland's most renowned, yet much more controversial, parkland courses. This is Druids Glen in Newtownmountkennedy, a tiny village just northeast of Glendalough, 'the valley of two lakes', in the heart of Wicklow, the 'Garden County'. In ways both remarkably alike and different from Killarney's courses, Druids Glen combines spectacular natural setting, design imagination, and landowner eccentricity. The result is a course that, although open for play only since 1995, has spearheaded a renewed interest in parkland courses in Ireland, both as an acknowledgment of the country's golfing heritage and as a reality check on the rapid diminishment of available sites for new links land courses in the face of prohibitive costs and stricter environmental regulations.

Cost, however, was not a factor in the building of Druids Glen. The man with the money was Hugo Flinn, who had amassed a fortune as a civil engineer building major projects throughout Africa. Like Cliff Roberts and Bobby Jones had done at Augusta National with Alister MacKenzie, Flinn headed a consortium of investors and hired two architects with whom he was familiar – Tom Craddock and Pat Ruddy, who had collaborated to build St Margaret's for him a few years earlier – and challenged them to build Ireland's best inland course. They may certainly have built its most beautiful, inviting ready comparisons with Augusta.

The site for Druids Glen is a spectacularly wooded site surrounding Woodstock House, an eighteenth-century Georgian country manor similar to many that exist throughout the region. Perhaps the most famous of these is Powerscourt in nearby Enniskerry at the foot of Great Sugar Loaf Mountain. Also dating to the mid-1700s,

Powerscourt oversees a 1,000-acre demesne, featuring waterfalls, an extraordinary gallery of outdoor statuary, and a series of terraced gardens that are the most impressive in Ireland. The Powerscourt gardens, emulating the formal conventions of their models from seventeenth- and eighteenth-century France and Italy, are demonstrations of affluence, designed to impose order over a vast landscape through transforming nature. As such, they aim to astonish visitors, not merely delight them. Druids Glen seems to have been motivated by the same goal. Like Berckman's Nursery, the land upon which Augusta National was built, the Woodstock Estate suggested that a golf course awaited to be fashioned there, not just discovered. Rounded hills, gentle undulations, wooded dells, a granite-walled canyon, and two clear mountain streams provided Craddock and Ruddy with the basic ingredients to shape their 'garden'. Calling on the services of landscape architect Jack O'Connor and agronomist James Lynch, the two designers developed a course that, in fact, represents a series of stages for their own skills, the features of the land, and the seasonal performances of the estate's flora. **Their achievement may be 'more beautiful than it is Irish', but it is dramatic and memorable.** [3] **It also facilitates two of the most delightful characteristics of golf itself – expectation and surprise.** For Druids Glen is a course, an experience, where there is always an expectation that something more is to be found in the garden/game, and that surprise – hopefully of a pleasant sort – awaits those discoveries.

An extraordinary set of par threes reveals all that Druids Glen is and aspires to be. The second is the only one of the four without water, a rarity on a course where water figures prominently on more than half of the holes. The tee shot on number two vaguely recalls the second shot to the green of the famous Road Hole, the seventeenth on the Old Course at St Andrews. For the player faces a mid to long-iron to a notoriously fast, right to left sloping green, with a bunker in the front cleft of the green and a stone wall and road behind the green. Like its inspiration at the Old Course, the road and wall are integral parts of the course, offering no relief.

#12, Druids Glen Golf Club, County Wicklow

The eighth and seventeenth at Druids Glen also reflect the great fun Craddock and Ruddy had in spending Flinn's money. Set in a natural amphitheatre on one of the lowest parts of the course, the 166-yard eighth recalls the sixteenth at Augusta. The tee shot must carry a pond to a severely sloping right to left green. Any ball not carrying far enough into the center of the green could easily roll off the left edge of the putting surface into the pond.

The seventeenth affords not even this much room for error. Completely surrounded by water, the island green – in fact, Ireland's first such green – obviously borrows from the terrifying seventeenth at the Tournament Player's Club in Sawgrass, Florida, architect Pete Dye's attempt to translate Stephen King to golf. The difference at Druids Glen is that the tee shot is considerably longer, over 200 yards from the tips.

The inspiration for the short twelfth, though, is more mystical than anything even Augusta National or the Old Course can provide. For this is the druids' own garden, a sanctuary of tall trees enveloping a nave-like green, protected front and right by a rock walled stream. Overlooking this scene, about halfway between the tee and the green, and tucked among a grove of sacred oaks, are the remains of a druid altar.

It is an absolutely stunning setting, yet somewhat compromised with two wholly artificial creations. For standing above the ancient altar with arms outstretched in a pose suggesting Leonardo's Christ in *The Last Supper* and wearing a less-than-approving expression on his face is a plastic, life-size image of a druid priest. And sprouting on the face of the elevated tee, but unseen unless players look back at the tee from the green, is a large Celtic cross perfectly arranged with dark green dwarf hebes and yellow spirea. These additions spell 'tourist', compelling cameras – and their owners – to focus less on the garden, than on the gardener.

No hole at Druids Glen, though, more fully demonstrates than the thirteenth how an architect can elaborate upon what the land provides, especially with virtually unlimited resources – and the twelve million Irish pounds (approximately $20 million) available to Craddock and Ruddy must have seen like that. If a principal purpose of a garden is to provide an extension of a dwelling, then one need only look to see what Flinn accomplished with Woodstock House to get a sense of the extremes to which he would go with his outdoors exhibition. After about £2 million in repairs, expansion, and renovation, Flinn not only had a handsome restoration project in his possession, but, more than likely, something that surpassed its original glory. Similarly, the goal at thirteen was not merely to 'improve' upon nature, but to introduce design where none previously existed.

The tee for the par four, 471-yard thirteenth is set hard against a granite cliff, high in the woods above the twelfth green. From the back markers, the player faces a narrow, diagonal fairway well below and running away from him, left to right. The fairway is set in a steeply bounded valley, defined by thick groves of tall chestnut and oak trees. Bordering the right side of the fairway is a creek that connects the pond on twelve with another that forms about 100 yards in front of the thirteenth green and continues around its entire left side. The exacting drive must carry the creek with a power fade, lest too straight a shot disappear in the woods across the fairway and too short a shot leave a perilous second of well over 200 yards, most of which is over water.

Like the grand gardens of the seventeenth century, this is a hole designed to effect astonishment.
As impressive as the design is, the process that created it might have been even more so. Flinn directed his architects to shear away an 80-foot high by 100-foot long section of the granite wall in order to accommodate the tee and provide an avenue to the fairway on the valley floor. Further, he re-routed the stream so that it crossed the fairway twice before emptying into the greenside pond, which he had excavated. 'Even the Japanese,' Ruddy asserts, 'would never have undertaken all this in order to build just one golf hole.'[4]

Hugo Flinn's goal, of course, was not to build just one great golf hole. Rather, it was to assemble a thrilling series of holes that would challenge the best players and leave all visitors to Druids Glen gasping for adjectives to describe the place. Aside from one too many plastic druids and an occasionally berserk horticultural moment, Druids Glen succeeds as a golf course and as a place of immense beauty.

Killarney and Druids Glen, of course, are not the only parkland courses in Ireland that provide great golf and gorgeous settings. An older group with such designer pedigrees as Alister MacKenzie, Harry Colt, Tom Simpson, and Fred Hawtree include, respectively, Cork, Belvoir Park, Carlow, and Malone. Extensive, mature woodlands in settings of rolling countryside characterise each of these courses. Each, too, has a distinctive physical asset – such as a quarry at Cork, or a 25 acre lake at Malone – that provides a foundation for the design. Although rich in golfing history, these courses are neither obsessed with rankings nor focused on tourists. **Yet, visitors are welcome for what the courses offer – classic parkland design, pleasant but unpretentious facilities, and a clear sense from the surrounding views and on-site hospitality that you are in Ireland.**

The latter point, however, cannot be said with the same degree of assurance about two recent and very high profile additions to the Irish parkland inventory. These are Mount Juliet, Jack Nicklaus' first design effort in Ireland, and the Kildare Hotel and Country Club, or, simply, The K Club, Arnold Palmer's second Irish project after Tralee. Yes, visitors are welcome at both places, but that is the point of both places. These are five-star luxury resorts and everything is geared to deliver on the expectations of quality and comfort – and price – of such establishments. Golf is the main attraction, but not the only draw.

The courses befit their environment. They are as ambitious and manicured as their accompanying hotel, spa, and equestrian complexes are tony and adorned. As such, they are formulaic to the point of distraction and indistinction, even including parading wildlife – pheasants at Mount Juliet and swans at The K Club. Both courses emphasise, indeed, celebrate, their manipulation of the landscape. Brochures proudly detail how tons of earth were moved, thousands of trees were planted, and dozens of water features were constructed. The point seems to be what money can do to the land, rather than what it can accomplish *with* the land. The result is something very pretty to behold, but more defined by universal high-end golf resort amenities than a distinctive Irish character.

These are places of paradox, promising an 'Irish experience', but offering something all too familiar to their primary intended clientele, that is, well-heeled Americans who regularly visit such oases in the United States. That the young K Club was selected as the site for the 2006 Ryder Cup, when the competition took place for the first time in Ireland, rather than a truly defining Irish course like Ballybunion, Portmarnock, or Royal County Down, seems almost incomprehensible. But the decision had much less to do with the quality of the course than the influence of Michael Smurfit and his millions (£32 million of which went into developing The K Club) and the global homogenisation of the game and its places of play. In other words, the pros, too, prefer five star hotels and perfect playing conditions to local B&Bs and links land quirkiness.

Seeing Mount Juliet and The K Club, which both opened a few years before Druids Glen, is important to gaining a greater a sense of what Craddock and Ruddy attempted to accomplish, and to avoid, in their work. Most clearly, Druids Glen acknowledges roots in, and respect for, the Irish parkland tradition that Killarney represents. And just as Killarney marked a transition in parkland design and concept from its predecessors, dating to the founding of the Curragh Golf Club in 1883, Druids Glen seems poised to do the same. With the completion of Ruddy's second course at Druids Glen, called Druids Heath, questions of affordability, audience, viability, and vision are again being asked, as they should be.

Notwithstanding the answers, one thing is certain. The 'gardens' of the game, like any garden, are never still. Even a corporate pair like Mount Juliet and The K Club are not ready-made. And they are never complete.

Along the banks of the River Liffey, #7, The K Club, County Kildare

No wonder the gods delight in such settings, so perfect both to provide pleasures and to harbour secrets.

CHAPTER SIX

Readers of the Game and Gods

I find that nature is the best architect.
I just try to dress up what the Good Lord provides.

Eddie Hackett, Irish golf architect (1995)

The secrets that golf reveals to the game's best are secrets
those players must discover for themselves.

Christy O'Connor, Sr, Irish professional golfer (1998)

YOU HIT THAT LIKE A GOD!

Michael 'Chuckie' O'Connell, Irish caddie (2000)

What makes golf in Ireland special? The links, above all, where the sky
and the sea collide with your dreams. This and the fact that there are still
uncrowded courses where you can just feel the land and the sky and the sea
and become part of that ethereal conglomeration.
'Tis to be like a god.

Pat Ruddy, Irish golf writer and editor, course designer and owner (2002)

Like no other game, golf is rooted in description and story and particularly rewards those who 'read' it well.

Perhaps, too, no other game provides as much to read or requires such close reading in order to understand its appeal or to play it well. The formal literature of the game – including an essential canon represented in the descriptive works of Bernard Darwin, Charles Blair Macdonald, Alister MacKenzie, and Herbert Warren Wind, and the instructional classics of Byron Nelson, Ben Hogan, Sam Snead, and Jack Nicklaus[1] – is only one expression of the reading that the game offers. Course guides and score cards are others, their numbers and symbols introducing the fields of play and recounting the stories of a round. The rules book provides an even deeper kind of read. It defines the conduct of the game and, in the closeness of its study and practice, the character of the player.

The knowledge that flows from Harvey Penick's *Little Red Book* or the tips in *Golf Digest* or the shelves of Sleeping Bear Press, however, achieves its fullest meaning within the context of personal experience.[2] For that allows a player to read *between* and *beneath* the lines of these narratives, to recall the stories that are within one's own memory and to apply them to both new and familiar situations. 'Reading' a putt or the wind or the lie of the ball requires knowledge of both what to look for and how to translate that knowledge into performance. The success of the translation depends upon the integrity of the narrative and the clarity of the read. What do we remember about a particular shot in a particular situation? Which narratives among the countless we have stored do we choose to recall? Is the experience within our memory true? **How we read is as important as what we read, for the act is informed by the perspectives and circumstances we bring to the reading.**

Such is the case in trying to read and understand the forces that have influenced and shaped the game in Ireland. For, though the game can be enjoyed at all skill levels, it can only be truly grasped as the layers of its nature and appeal are peeled away and considered. Different lenses – those of the architect, player, caddie, and writer – reveal Irish golf and each makes its own unique contribution to the complete picture.

SAINT EDDIE

There are two eras in Irish golf course architecture – B.E. and A.E. Before Eddie (Hackett) and After Eddie.

If there was not void before gentle Eddie, there certainly was not wholeness. Scotsmen serving in the military and English aristocrats tending their grand estates brought the game to Ireland in the late nineteenth century. They also brought their own course designers – pioneers in the emerging profession of golf architecture like Old Tom Morris, Alister MacKenzie, Harry Shapland Colt, and Willie Park. These men had honed their skills and styles in Scotland and England while elevating course design to something more purposeful than customarily agreed upon starting and finishing points with several rabbit holes and sheep-scraped bunkers along the way. In the 25 years before the outbreak of the First World War in 1914, over 100 courses were built in Ireland and this foursome had a hand in many of the most important, including Lahinch, Rosapenna, Portstewart, Royal County Down, Rosses Point, Royal Belfast, Royal Dublin, and Royal Portrush. None of those courses, however, were built for the Irish commoner or revenue-providing visitors.

Eddie Hackett was an unlikely messiah in transforming Irish golf design and the golfing business. Born in a Dublin pub in 1910, he struggled through an *Angela's Ashes*-like childhood of poverty and illness, including long periods of hospitalisation to treat tuberculosis. His doctors did permit young Eddie to play golf for the exercise and the fresh air and he enthusiastically embraced the game. As a teenager, he landed a job as a club maker at Royal Dublin and continued to work on his game over those historic links on North Bull Island that Harry Colt had redesigned after

Eddie Hackett

the war. Rising to the level of assistant pro, Hackett stayed at Royal Dublin until 1939, when, at age 29, he was offered the head professional position at Portmarnock.

Setbacks to his health (he had a kidney removed in 1936 and suffered a bout of meningitis in 1954) and economic well-being (a failed non-golf business venture in the early 1950s) dimmed Hackett's prospects again. A devout Catholic, however, he was buoyed by his faith and devotion to the game. He also came to realise how many friends he had gained over the years. Some of these friends came to his rescue in 1960, when, attempting to capitalise on the excitement of Portmarnock hosting the World Cup, the Golfing Union of Ireland asked him to give a series of golfing clinics across the country in order to awaken his countrymen to the joys of the game. In the midst of this assignment, he was offered another – to design a course – the first of 85 he would eventually lay out. All of them are in Ireland.

There is a simple eloquence to Hackett's courses that reflect the character of the man. A deeply religious person, who attended daily Mass and aspired to emulate the modest virtues of the good man in Thomas Aquinas' *The Imitation of Christ,* Hackett recognised a spiritual presence in the land. When Eddie proclaimed a site as 'blessed by God', he did not seek to distinguish it from less attractive locations. He truly meant it as a universal acknowledgment of the hand of Providence. Accordingly, he approached each design project with keen respect for what the land provided, and a sense of responsibility not to intrude upon it. The sites for his courses were not stages for an architect's ego. Rather, eschewing contrivance and trickery, Hackett's designs are remarkably straightforward and rhythmic, achieving harmony with the natural features and flows of the landscape, not challenging or contradicting them. Even one of his later efforts, Carne, located on the isolated Atlantic coast of County Mayo and described as 'Ballybunion on steroids', looks like it was discovered, not placed, among the towering sand dunes of its tumultuous setting.

Hackett's commitment to golf in Ireland, though, went beyond his respect for nature and his exclusive focus on designing courses in his native land. These behaviours were expressions of his passion for the game itself and a desire to bring golf to his countrymen, more for their own pleasure than as an agent of economic stimulus. The latter is a development only within the last 25 years. 'Eddie is the unsung hero of Irish golf,' says Pat Ruddy, Ireland's leading golf journalist and the designer of The European Club, a links very much in keeping with Hackett's minimalist design philosophy.[3] 'At a time when there was no money, Eddie Hackett travelled the high-ways and byways of Ireland. Half the people playing golf in Ireland are doing so because of Eddie Hackett.'

From Connemara to Waterville, Enniscorthy to Enniscrone, Donegal to Ceann Sibeal, Hackett designed courses, as great as they are lyrical, for a small fee, but a grand vision. 'Oh, Eddie Hackett is a saint, you know,' proclaimed Father Peter Waldron, who spearheaded the effort to enlist Hackett's services in 1970 to build a golf course at Clifden on the rocky western coast of the Connemara peninsula.[4] Hackett's glowing assessment of the site, and next-to-nothing fee, strengthened the community's resolve to see it through. The result is a course entirely built by the locals and one that has delivered on its promise of extraordinary golf and better economic times.

If not the first saint or golf architect to leave his mark on Ireland, Eddie Hackett was surely the first Irish architect to earn a halo. He died in December 1996, working on new projects to the very end. **An Irish original, Eddie Hackett prayed for divine guidance in all that he did. The wonderful courses he planted throughout the country affirm a life of spiritual connection and favour.**

HIMSELF

In Ireland, wrote E. Estyn Evans nearly a half century ago, 'geography counts for more than genes'.[5] This testimony to the power of place explains the great affection that Ireland bestows on her heroes, especially those who wear her colours bravely on the international stage. After they had *lost* to Spain on penalty kicks in the first round of soccer's 2002 World Cup, the Irish national team came home from South Korea to a hero's welcome with over 100,000 fans turning out in Dublin's Phoenix Park to celebrate their play. One can only imagine the response if they had advanced in the tournament. Golf, of course, through its several tours and internationally-oriented competitions, like the Ryder Cup, Walker Cup, and the World Cup, affords just such an arena for glory. **No golfer brought more glory to his homeland than a wristy-swinging ball striker from Galway who would earn his friends' admiration as the 'Great Man', or more simply, 'Himself' – Christy O'Connor, Sr.**

In the small world of Irish golf, O'Connor would call home the same club, Royal Dublin, where Eddie Hackett started his career in golf. Thirty-five years old in 1959 when he arrived from Knocknacarra as the club professional at Saint Eddie's old haunts, Christy was the toast of Ireland. Less than ten years into a late-starting professional career, he had not only established himself as a force on the British and European tours with victories in such major events as the Dunlop Masters (1956) and European PGA Match Play (1957) tournaments, but he had also propelled Irish golf to the pinnacle of international competition. For, in 1958, Himself had teamed with 'The Brad' – the veteran Wicklow pro, Harry Bradshaw – to win the Canada Cup (now World Cup) at the Club de Golf in Mexico City. The victory over such stellar international teams as Sam Snead and Ben Hogan of the United States and Gary Player and Harold Henning of South Africa brought O'Connor and Bradshaw home as conquering heroes, greeted by adoring thousands at Shannon Airport and in their hometowns. The World Cup triumph was an achievement the Irish would not repeat again until 1997, when Padraig Harrington and Paul McGinley rallied from a two-shot final day deficit and won the world championship on the Ocean Course at Kiawah Island, South Carolina.

When O'Connor and Bradshaw won the World Cup in 1958, though, the quality of Irish golf was barely a rumour beyond those few international visitors who had experienced the pleasures of the country's links. Suddenly, though, similar to what John Sutherland's play at the 1907 British Amateur had accomplished for Scotland's Royal Dornoch and Bobby Jones' emergence in the 1920s had done for golf in the American South, golfing pilgrims started streaming to the training grounds of the Gaelic champions. The great victory of the new pro at Royal Dublin set the stage for the architectural career of the club's former employee, Eddie Hackett, to take off as communities throughout the country looked to build courses to breed future Irish champions and bank new tourist dollars.

Like Hackett, O'Connor has been proclaimed a national treasure throughout the land for what he achieved on the land. Ten times Irish professional champion and the winner of 60 other tournaments worldwide, Himself competed in the World Cup fifteen times and played on ten consecutive Ryder Cup teams from 1955 to 1973.

Only Britain's Nick Faldo, with eleven Ryder Cup appearances, has represented the Europeans more often in the biennial matches. Although Christy never won a 'major', he finished in the top 25 at the British Open 19 out of the 23 times he participated in the event. His strongest showing was a runner-up finish at Royal Birkdale in 1965, two strokes behind Peter Thomson.[6]

By all accounts, O'Connor never passed on a pint or a game. 'Somebody once said that every Irishman wanted to buy Christy O'Connor a drink,' Himself recalled in his autobiography, 'and that most had succeeded.'[7] *'I will not deny I like my few jars,'* admitted O'Connor, but he explained that a few pints after a hard day's golf was his 'cushion against the physically and mentally exhausting life style of the tournament circuits of the world'. He even argued that a 'warming Guinness in the cooler weather or a soothing ale when it was hot' gave him an advantage, for such pleasures were a relatively benign way to relax compared to 'the other evils that stalk those living half their lives out of a suitcase'. 'Mind you,' he said, 'the recuperative occasion of golf's nineteenth hole oftimes brought me its own troubles.' But to suggest that he was 'in more bar room brawls than Wyatt Earp ... is pretty much wide of the mark'.

Both his 'jarring' and his golfing heroics endeared him even more, and in equal measure, to his countrymen. He won, for example, the Dunlop Masters at Prestwick in 1956 by overcoming a six-shot deficit in the final round, took the Carrolls International Tournament at Royal Dublin in 1966 with an eagle-birdie-eagle finish, and thoroughly trounced Dow Finsterwall, 7&6, in the Ryder Cup matches at Lindrick in 1957 to lead the Britain-Ireland side to its first victory since 1933. Particularly when he competed in Ireland, 'O'C' drew upon the affection and support of his countrymen, including their prayers, the special contribution of his 'black pack', the Irish clergy who marched in his galleries. His fellow citizens hailed him as a true Irish hero, Cúchulainn-like in the wild legends that his temper, pub exploits, and golfing achievements inspired. **'He was a well-balanced Irishman,'** summarised one acquaintance. **'He had chips on both shoulders.'**[8]

Christy O'Connor

He also had a game like Hogan's, rooted in the land, literally, in the dirt. He practised incessantly – 'there were not enough daylight hours for me to practice'[9] – so as to groove his natural swing, beating balls off beaches and hardpan in any weather condition, and always with a purpose. No less than Hogan, O'Connor admitted to being consumed by golf. And certainly no less than Saint Eddie, the Great Man's manner and obsession earned him the status of folk hero in Ireland.

CHUCKIE

'Are you black?' asked the Irish caddie of his player after he had hit a shot poorly and then uttered an audible curse at himself. Startled, the player wondered what it was about his fair complexion and sandy hair that could possibly prompt such a question. 'What?' he asked, somewhat defensively. 'Are you black?' repeated the caddie. "No, I'm not,' declared the player, now a bit irritated. 'What do you mean?' 'Are you Tiger Woods?' answered the caddie. The player now understood. He was not black. He was not Tiger Woods. He was not perfect.

Michael O'Connell, nicknamed 'Chuckie' because his own golf swing resembled that of a local County Kerry player of the same name, has been developing his repertoire of folk wisdom and story to amuse and guide his clients for over 50 years, ever since he first slung a player's bag across his back at age twenty in 1948. Back then the few coins he earned as a caddie were vital contributions to his family's survival, for the post-war years were not easy ones for most in Ireland, especially those living in the rural western counties.

Although not a combatant during the Second World War, Ireland had suffered severe food and fuel shortages that persisted well after the German surrender. Despairing of their prospects for employment and economic advancement, 80 per cent of Chuckie's peers, that is, those children born in Ireland in the 1930s, would emigrate before they were out of their twenties. Ireland had not suffered such population losses since the 1880s. The bitterness that these émigrés directed at their government for its inability to provide for its people further contributed to the depressed spirit and economy of the country. An entire post-war generation grew up as children of the 'sick man' of Europe.

Although Ireland joined the European Economic Community in 1973, it did not fully throw off the symptoms of its social malaise and depressed economic conditions until the 1980s. But buoyed by EEC funding, particularly in infrastructure development, enormous telecommunications investments, and convenient, affordable air travel and its prosperous consequences for the tourist industry, Ireland entered the twenty-first century transformed as the 'Celtic Tiger'.

Chuckie has witnessed the full transformation and his perspective from the caddie yard reflects the development of golf in Ireland as much as it chronicles his own passages. Unlike caddies in Scotland and England, who can trace their bag-toting roots to the late eighteenth century, caddies in Ireland were never reviled as social outcasts.[10] The pervasive poverty of the island did not permit the kind of class-based judgments that existed in the aristocratic golfing circles across the Irish Sea about the respectability, or not, of seemingly unskilled manual work. Besides, caddying was about *working the land* and in a country which, as late as 1960, employed less than fifteen per cent of its population in the industrial sector, no work on the land was considered ignoble.

Among the most senior of Ireland's caddies at age 80 in 2006, Chuckie has long since overcome any regret in not joining the exodus of his countrymen to America many years ago. Although he has used trolleys in recent years to haul bags around Tralee – a battery-powered one that leads him and a hand-pulled second trolley crab-like over the fairways and dunes – **he has not lost a step in the sharpness of his conversation or the skills of reading greens and clubbing his player.**

In many respects, Chuckie is a transitional figure in the world of the Irish caddie. His age suggests connection to the stereotype of an ancient bag carrier, a gnarled, idiosyncratic veteran of the links whose penchant for spinning tales was matched only by his capacity for quaffing pints. **Chuckie's knowledge of the game, however, and his uncanny ability to 'work the tools', that is, quickly size up a player's strengths and weaknesses, including his attitude towards the game, reflects a craftsman at work.** It is not surprising that so many of the new breed of Irish caddies are fine players themselves, often members of the clubs where they 'carry the sticks'. In this regard, such caddies echo a rich tradition that includes a trio of Scotsmen – Old Tom Morris, Jamie Anderson, and Allan Robertson – who all started their golfing lives as caddies and left lasting imprints on the game as playing professionals and architects.

No less than Saint Eddie and Himself, Chuckie – and the tribe of caddies he represents – adds colour and personality to the distinctive world of Irish golf. **Quiet pride and a gentle spirituality befitting the land he works particularly underscore Chuckie's charms.** Whether advising a player on the first tee to place his game in his trust, praising a fine shot as 'godlike', explaining a rare lost ball as 'captured by the gods', or serenading a foursome with a rich baritone rendition of 'The Rose of Tralee', Chuckie is not just the dean of Irish caddies, but their model. No wonder he is affectionately known at Tralee as 'Chuckie the legend'.

Perhaps, though, the most important quality that Chuckie at Tralee and his brethren throughout Ireland bring to a round is memorability. Understanding both the design features of a course and how they will handle any weather condition or any player's game, the caddie evokes the memory within a golfing landscape that can be traced to its architect – human or divine. His contemporary translation of such vision and intent insures a memorable experience for his players. **For like any good oracle, and there has been none better than Chuckie, the Irish caddie offers wisdom that is both particular and universal – and remembrance of a journey wonderfully enhanced through the pleasure of his company.**

Chuckie O'Connell at #12, Tralee Golf Club, County Kerry in 2002

SINCERELY, IN GOLF

No one has more thoughtfully or passionately chronicled the Irish golfing scene than Pat Ruddy. For nearly 40 years, beginning as a freelance writer and graduating to five broadsheet pages a week with the Dublin *Evening Herald* in the 1960s, Ruddy has projected his voice particularly through the pages of the *Golfer's Companion*, a magazine which he launched in 1973. Like the most popular golf periodicals, the *Golfer's Companion* offers its fair share of player profiles, instructional features, course photos, and tournament coverage. But, unlike the others, Ruddy's magazine devotes considerably greater depth and insight to matters more philosophical and historical. The result is a publication with a niche and purpose that underscores Ruddy's contribution to mass production golf news and musings when the game was just beginning to take hold in Ireland in a modern sense.

No messages have been more central to Ruddy's writing and the other dimensions of his career in golf than that the game is fun, it should be accessible, and that it has a heritage worth knowing and preserving. More often than not, his projects and pursuits have brought all of these elements together.

Hailing from County Mayo in the northwest, Ruddy enjoyed an almost idyllic golfing youth. His home course was Harry Colt's masterpiece at Rosses Point on Drumcliff Bay. As a junior member of the club, he had ready access to one of Ireland's most beautiful and historic links. As his career as a golf journalist developed, though, Ruddy realised how limited the opportunities were for his countrymen, even those of some means, to find places to play. His desire to address this situation coincided with a campaign to build public courses that the Golfing Union of Ireland had launched in the 1960s following the World Cup at Portmarnock. Taking up the cause, Ruddy announced in his newspaper column the formation of 'The Homeless Golfers' with the goal of providing golfing opportunities for those who did not have club memberships.

The response to his call astounded Ruddy. Within a few months, nearly a thousand 'homeless' golfers had come forward, their numbers eventually swelling to more than twice that. Assisted by some key members and secretaries of Dublin's clubs, they found themselves teeing it up on many of the finest courses in the area for the cost of about one euro, albeit, with 6.00a.m. starting times. No one complained. Five years after the campaign began, the Dublin area opened its first truly public course and Ruddy's 'homeless' legions reorganised themselves as the Dublin and County Golf Club. Ruddy helped finance a clubhouse for the formerly 'homeless' through a second mortgage on his home. Says Ruddy about this chapter in Irish golf, it 'just goes to prove that getting to the first tee is the main problem in this game'. [11]

Ruddy has not only been helping golfers get to the first tee, but he has been providing them with an ever-growing portfolio of some of the finest first tees throughout the country. Beginning with an invitation in 1971 to design a nine-hole layout at Castlecomer, a few miles north of Kilkenny, Ruddy counts some 30 courses among

Pat Ruddy in a bunker on #2 at The
European Club, County Wicklow in 2007

those he has either developed from the outset or helped expand or renew. The completed jewels in his chest of Irish designs include the Glashedy Links at Ballyliffin, The European Club (his self-proclaimed 'diamond'), Druids Glen, and St Margaret's. His most recent works include a second course at Newtownmountkennedy (Druids Heath), a second links at Rosapenna, and substantial redesigns of the venerable links of Portsalon and Donegal. Although proud of all of these efforts, he is particularly pleased that Castlecomer asked him to set out a second nine where his design career began. 'Isn't it nice,' he says about this invitation, 'to have the circle complete itself from 1971 through 2001.' A mark of the man is that he accepted no fee for this work.

Ruddy's enthusiasm for 'the simple pursuit of a ball across a pasture' has been manifest in ways both traditional and unorthodox. His particular devotion to links land courses reflects his serious respect for the history of the game and its earliest pioneers. The latter, he says, 'still stalk those fairways invisible only to those who do not feel'. Yet, like his campaign for the 'homeless' golfer, he has promoted the game in light-hearted fashion, too. Arranging the use of a military airfield through a golfing friend, the Irish Minister of Defence, for example, he invited Liam Higgins to hit away and the result was the World's Long Drive Record. This was followed by the World's Long Drive Over Water at Waterville, set by Paul Leonard, and an entire family of similarly whimsical achievements.

After 50 years of engagement in the business and pleasure of golf, Ruddy stands at the crossroads of the game in Ireland. His current design projects are among an entirely new generation of courses that are opening in his country. Those who are affixing their signatures to these venues constitute a virtual 'who's who' in the world of golf – Arnold Palmer, Greg Norman, Jack Nicklaus, Christy O'Connor, Jr., Mark O'Meara, Colin Montgomery, Seve Ballesteros, and Nick Price. Some courses, like Palmer's second course at The K Club, Norman's at Doonbeg in County Clare, and Ron Kirby's new layout at Hog's Head near Waterville, will be at the high end of the fee spectrum. Others, like Ruddy's at Rosapenna, focus less on the cost to the player than the connection to, and celebration of, the design genius of Old Tom Morris, James Braid, Harry Vardon, and Eddie Hackett. Hanging in the balance are such critical issues as the availability of land, the affordability of play, and the relationship between the purposes brought to playing a game and the profits sought in providing it.

The world of golf has been blessed not only through the many expressions of Ruddy's work for the game in Ireland, but also his articulation of a more universal message. 'Get into the links and let it get into you,' he advises.[12] A simple invitation and as eloquent and heartfelt as the closing of his letters, '*Sincerely, in Golf.*'

At the very beginning of Irish history, it would seem, there was already nostalgia for an earlier time. There was a strong sense that current events could be justified – or explained – by knowledge of past events.

David W. McCullough, *Wars of the Irish Kings* (2000)

CHAPTER SEVEN

A Fearful Look:

Kinsale and the Future of Golf in Ireland

When the gods of golf are at play in the seaside dunes, they are at their most vexatious and amusing best.

Pat Ruddy, Irish golf writer, designer and developer (2000)

A rain shelter on the Old Course,
Ballybunion Golf Club, County Kerry

There are many approaches to Kinsale. Whether by land or sea, the

routes to this port town overlooking the estuary of the River Bandon on Ireland's southern coast are among

the most beautiful in the entire country. The coast road from County Kerry meanders southeast into County

Cork past a succession of jagged peninsulas and rugged islands, large bays and deep inlets, defining the untamed

Atlantic coast of the Munster province. A procession of ancient market towns such as Bantry, Skibbereen, and

Clonakilty sit at the heads of various waterways and reveal their once vital strategic importance through the

IRA memorials, castle ruins, and other archaeological sites that mark the landscape.

Out of Cork, the Republic's second largest city, a shorter and more travelled way to Kinsale heads southwest through the valleys of the once densely wooded hills where druids performed their rites well before St Finbar in the seventh century and the Vikings in the ninth settled upon the marshy island between two branches of the River Lee. Upon reaching Inishannon village, the Kinsale road turns due south and accompanies the River Bandon to the sea. Its many bends reveal one postcard view after another, each, it seems, complemented with its own weather and mood.

Yet, there is unity within the transformations of atmosphere and scenery. Robert Lynd, writing a century ago, thought that the key element which provided a 'personality' to Ireland, that which forged a connection among the vastly different Irish countrysides, was 'the glory of light'.[1] Along the River Bandon road, a multi-karat morning mist touches gently, brilliantly, equally on all it enfolds, especially a myriad of white-washed farmhouses and cottages of all imaginable shapes and sizes that dot the slopes and plains like yachts at anchor on a green sea.

Real yachts and all manner of sail and sporting boat that come for the sun and blue shark do lie at anchor in Kinsale Harbour. Located within one of the most sheltered bays in the south of Ireland, the harbour is the centerpiece of the well-heeled and self-styled 'capital of the Irish *Cote d'Azur*'. Especially for those who arrive by sea, passing by the steep slopes and cave-riddled sea cliffs of Old Head and Frower Point, the town is stunningly beautiful as it comes into view. It flows gently to the sea from an encirclement of lush hills, down narrow lanes lined with meticulously preserved eighteenth-century houses and brightly painted shop fronts, their window boxes and street stanchions bursting with flowers in full bloom. It appears, in fact, too perfect, an over-the-top entry in the country's annual Tidy Town competition – which it has won consistently. Yet, it obviously offers what tourists and a growing list of celebrity residents want – something that looks only like Ireland.

An historical approach to the area reveals a violent past that encompasses the internecine wars of the ancient Irish kings, waves of invaders (both real and mythological), the nineteenth-century Fenian Movement, and the Civil

War of the 1920s. The defining event in Kinsale's history, though, one that had far-reaching consequences for all of Ireland, occurred on Christmas Eve 1601. In a brief, fierce battle that climaxed a campaign of several years, an English army of 7,000 troops, commanded by Charles Blount, Lord Mountjoy, routed an Irish army led by Hugh O'Neill, the Earl of Tyrone. The English then forced the surrender of the town and its garrison, some 3,500 Spanish soldiers, who had been sent to Kinsale by King Phillip III to aid the cause of a fellow Catholic aligned against the Protestant Tudors.

The destruction of the most powerful Irish force ever assembled against the English had immediate and long-lasting effects. English authority, although still occasionally challenged, triumphed at the expense of the old Gaelic and set back the cause of Irish nationalism for many generations. Kinsale became an English-only town, where the Irish were not allowed to live again until the late eighteenth century. The leading Irish rebels throughout the country scurried for their safety. O'Neill lingered in Ireland until 1607, but then gave up the cause and lived out his days in Rome. Hugh Roe O'Donnell, O'Neill's son-in-law and co-commander during the Kinsale campaign, fled to Spain. Their departure along with their families, retainers, and other lords constituted 'the flight of the earls'. It signalled the end of the power of the old Irish royalty, the beginning of a period of Irish emigration, and the birth of Protestant Ulster. No more poignant summary of the sense of loss and change after the battle of Kinsale exists than that provided by an unknown Donegal Franciscan in the early-seventeenth-century compendium, *Annals of the Kingdoms of Ireland:* 'Prowess and valour, prosperity and affluence, nobleness and chivalry, dignity and renown, hospitality and generosity, bravery and protection, devotion and pure religion, of the Island, were lost in this engagement.'[2]

It is particularly ironic that O'Donnell arrived at the court of Spain with a copy of the *Lebor Gabala* in his possession. For it was this ancient text that chronicled the waves of Irish invasions – immigrations – from the descendants of Noah to the sons of Mil. The story of the latter, of course, was how the children of 'the soldier from Spain' had defeated the Tuatha De Danann, thereby becoming the most immediate ancestors of the Irish. If Phillip was

Aerial view of the Old Head Golf Links, County Cork

listening to this story, he certainly was not buying its implications about kinship and destiny. He had lost interest in Ireland as a place in which to wage war against Protestantism and looked elsewhere, most notably the European continent and the struggle that would become the Thirty Years War.

In closing a chapter of the 'Irish Question', Kinsale both completed the rings of Irish history and mythology and transformed them. Gods and kings would continue to exert their influence, but storybook and song, rather than battlefield and court, became the places of their dwelling. If Kinsale is the dividing line between Ireland's idyllic and post-heroic historical eras, then it should not be surprising how the region is influencing, and transforming, other aspects of the country's culture – especially *haute*, like cuisine, conspicuous excess, and golf. For located 7 miles southwest of the harbour and situated on top of the Old Head promontory, a diamond-shaped tract of about 220 acres, connected to the rest of the peninsula and the mainland by a spectacular natural bridge, is a golf course that defies imagination – and nature. **This is the Old Head Golf Links.**

And there is nothing like it anywhere on this planet.

In the first place, it is built on a spit of land whose awesome beauty is matched only by its historical significance. According to Ptolemy, an Alexandrian Greek geographer and astronomer who wrote in the middle of the second century, the Erainn, the most important pre-Christian dynasty in Munster, established settlements on Old Head as far back as the third century BC. Perhaps even earlier, for the Erainn were the descendants of the goddess Eiru, the namesake of Ireland. It was she who figured prominently in the negotiations between the Tuatha De Danaan and the Milesians that effected the division of Ireland between the peoples of the surface and the spirits beneath it. Lending more evidence to the bond between the mythological and the historical, physical traces of the Erainn remain in scattered ruins, among the walls of ancient castles and lighthouses that were built by successive occupants of these venerable grounds. To recognise this heritage, Old Head has been designated as a national monument.

Looking north towards the mainland along the west side of the Old Head peninsula,
Old Head Golf Links, County Cork

So how could a golf course be built on top of it? It seems as unlikely a prospect as someone buying Valley Forge National Historic Park in order to design eighteen holes among the ruins and relics of the Continental Army's Revolutionary War encampment and to convert George Washington's headquarters into the clubhouse.

The pair who accomplished this feat were the brothers O'Connor, John and Patrick, successful real estate developers and entrepreneurs with a sense that upscale golf and the Kinsale tourist business were made for each other. Whether the locals knew what the O'Connors had in mind when they purchased the land for about €200,000 and then started hauling in thousands of tons of topsoil to cover the exposed, rocky soil is hotly debated. Patrick assigns lingering animosity to the €7 million project – and the €295 green fees in 2007, the highest in Ireland – to those who lost the legal battles to prevent it. As for the locals, now that the course has been open since 1997,

Looking north towards the mainland along the east (Kinsale) side of the
Old Head peninsula, Old Head Golf Links, County Cork

Patrick simply dismisses them. 'Don't need 'em,' he explains. 'They don't play Old Head – can't afford it. It wasn't built for them anyway.' Lord Mountjoy must be smiling wherever he is.

The international golf set for whom Old Head was built, though, could not care less about the politics behind the project or the fees to experience it. They come in droves (and helicopters) to see what the O'Connors fashioned with the project's chief architect, Ron Kirby, and a host of Irish golf consultants, including the dean of Irish golf architects, Eddie Hackett, Waterville's head professional Liam Higgins, agronomist Paddy Merrigan, and the country's greatest amateur champion, Joe Carr of Portmarnock. Sitting in the pub room of the Patrick Byrne-designed clubhouse, which blends perfectly into a rocky slope in the style of Frank Lloyd Wright, visitors have glorious panoramic views of the course beneath them and the nineteenth century lighthouse at its farthest point.

For those about to play, the sight is spectacularly inviting. **For those who have completed their rounds, the experience is already turning mythic.**

The course begins in an innocent and minimalist fashion with a gentle, slightly uphill, dogleg right par four of 420 yards from the back tees. Yet, one is immediately aware that, for all of its oceanfront exposure and name, this is not a links course. The imported topsoil lacks the springy quality of true links land and does not yield the hard rolls or the distinctive, sensually pleasing crunching sound made from a well-struck ball off of crisp turf on a compacted sandy base. The bunkering, especially in the fairways, is also rather ordinary, lacking the ruggedness, depth, and penal placement that define links courses. This is more accurately headlands golf, or even cliff top. The first hole, though, provides little clue how the standard for a headlands course – perhaps best represented in Pebble Beach and its stretch of holes along the 150-foot high cliffs of Carmel Bay – is about to change.

From the first green, a pathway leads to the second tee past the ruins of a seventeenth-century lighthouse and an early nineteenth century signal tower. These are impressive, the real thing, and they erase somewhat the bad impression from the *faux* holed standing stone near the first tee. The sight that greets upon reaching the second tee, though, transforms players to another level of reality. For perched on the edge of a cliff 300 feet above the sea at Kitchen Point is a narrow shelf and the tee blocks. The seaward view to the east, towards Kinsale Harbour, is dizzying; the view down the fairway towards the green, the lighthouse, the Atlantic is absolutely dazzling. A tumbling, falling fairway, guarded by shallow bunkers on both sides, bends sharply left around a sheer drop-off called the Gun Hole. Any place left of the fairway is not a good place to be, especially in search of a golf ball. The green is just as precariously placed as the tee, hard against the lateral drop to eternity. **Welcome to Old Head.**

Nine of Old Head's holes play completely along the cliffs and two others have set their tees at the cliff's edge. **Just when you swear you have played the most spectacular golf hole in the world, you move on to another**

and your jaw drops another notch and your vocabulary strains for another expression for 'unreal' **and** 'you've got to be kidding me!' The short third, for example, only 153 yards, seems about to slide over the cliffs at any moment. The aptly named 'Razor's Edge' fourth repeats the Wagnerian design concepts of the second and continues the journey around the southeastern perimeter of the course, bringing play to the foot of the lighthouse at the tip of the peninsula. It is not very comforting to know that it was from this vantage point that the lighthouse keeper watched the British passenger liner *Lusitania* sink just a few miles offshore on 7 May 1915, after a single torpedo from a German U-boat burst into it. 1,198 people, including 128 Americans, lost their lives when the great ship went down in only eighteen minutes. The resulting outcry against the 'massacre of innocents' pushed the United States closer to entry in the First World War.

Today, Old Head's casualties are mainly adjectives and golf balls. There are just not enough of the former to describe the course or a sufficient supply of the latter to get around it if the winds are up, as they usually are, and your game is not. Three places, in particular, where the superlatives flow and the balls disappear quickly, albeit, heroically, in any weather condition are the tee shots on the seventh and the twelfth and the approach to the par five seventeenth.

Yes, the course actually gets stronger and more dazzling as it goes on.

From the back tees on seven, among the ruins of the 1600's lighthouse, the shot is 191 yards to a kidney shaped green, surrounded by bunkers. It offers the most exhilarating tee shot on the eastern side of the peninsula and merits the same description which William Shakespeare provided for a similarly frightening location west of Dover, namely, 'a place whose high and bending head looks fearfully on the confined deep'.[4] **The entire Old Head ensemble is here – ancient ruins, vertiginous**

views, sparkling sea, cascading cliffs, and laugh-out-loud wonder.

The most spectacular tee shot on the entire course, though, is from the championship markers on the dogleg left, 498-yard twelfth. On the more exposed western side of the peninsula, the tee sits on a sunken shelf carved into the cliffside several hundred feet above Ringagurteen Point. The drive to the narrow, semi-hidden fairway requires a thrilling transoceanic carry towards distant castle towers, over the coves and caves of the sheer cliffs. It is a terrifying shot, whether the striker is familiar with the hole or not. Number seventeen is also a par five that tumbles majestically, magnetically, towards a tiny green perched above Coosgorm Cove, near the very end of the Old Head spit. The approach on this 626-yard rollercoaster affords another all-world view of the lighthouse and beyond. In case one has doubts about the challenge, the course guide notes that this is 'a difficult hole and requires considerable thought for second and third shot'. Requiring thought of any kind at this point in a round seems particularly cruel and unusual punishment. Almost as incongruous were the life-size sculptures of John Belushi and

#4, Old Head Golf Links, County Cork

Dan Aykroyd's comedic creations, the Blues Brothers, which sat on the clubhouse veranda overlooking play on the two finishing holes for a time after the course first opened. Now, what was that all about!?

But, in many respects, the notion of Jake and Elwood surveying the grounds may be a metaphor for the course. The question about their former presence is the same one that nags upon finishing a round: what is Old Head all about?

Joe Carr has described the course as 'the eighth wonder of the world in golfing terms'. There is no doubt that no course, anywhere, surpasses its dramatic setting. It is thrilling to play and completely lives up to its promotional billing – 'from the aeons of time … spectacular beyond belief'. But its memorability is not necessarily in the marriage of brilliant design, shot-making requirements, and aesthetics that defines places like Cypress Point, Royal Dornoch or Shinnecock. Unlike them, Old Head leaves many players with an awkward emptiness, a sense of delight to be sure, but not necessarily a compelling desire to tee it up again. **A truly great course should bring you back for more than the views.**

Neither is it the sheer audacity of the O'Connors to have built a golf course at this location nor some of its cute contrivances, like the fake dolmen just off the ninth fairway, that account for the uneasiness. It is something deeper and more disturbing, something that recalls Shakespeare's description of the place as fearful. But it is not the dizzying views over the cliffs that cause disquiet. It is the troubling sense that Old Head represents the future of golf in Ireland – over the top green fees and uniformed caddies, tarmacadam cart paths and roaming bar carts, gated entrances and year-in-advance reservation requirements, foursomes from Bakersfield rather than singles from Ballinspittle, pro shops with more crystal and cashmere than Switzer & Co., menus with more imported wines and bottled waters than native stouts and whiskeys.

Just as Waterville connects to the heroic origins of Irish history, mythology, and golf, Old Head and Kinsale suggest the tony dimensions of a new economy and value system. How far the 'Celtic Tiger' roams from its own history and traditional culture will be among the most interesting and important developments to watch in Ireland as the twenty-first century unfolds. Among the clues will be the lessons that others draw from Old Head and Kinsale.

Yet, there are those who have already determined that Old Head is not the only direction for the future of Irish golf. Among the leaders in the Irish golfing world who hold this view is Pat Ruddy and he has done more than just rail against 'drop-from-heaven type' courses – well funded, commercially-driven ventures that look impressive, but fall short of the promise of great golf.[5] He has 'gone back to the future' for his inspiration and constructed an impressive counterpoint.

His argument, The European Club, opened on St Stephen's Day 1992, with the distinction of being the first new bona fide links course to be built on the Irish Sea coast in the twentieth century. With his keen sense of history, Ruddy undoubtedly knew that the last such course to open, Portmarnock, did so on the same day 98 years earlier. Located at Brittas Bay, about 40 miles south of Dublin, it sits among the sea grasses and dramatic dunes of a muscular stretch of coastland that easily conjures up images of Ballybunion and Waterville. It is the fulfillment of two lifetime goals of Ruddy – to design, develop, and own a world class links course, and to affirm the heritage and distinctiveness of such courses in Ireland. He has succeeded on both accounts.

A student and promoter of golf nearly all of his life, Ruddy brought to the wild site on Brittas Bay relatively little personal experience in golf course construction, but a deep appreciation of design genius. He aimed to borrow the principles, and some of the tricks, from such old masters as Old Tom Morris, Harry Colt, and Alister MacKenzie and to work in some of the ideas from the leading twentieth-century architects whom he also admired. The latter group included Donald Ross, Pete Dye, and Robert Trent Jones, Sr. But Ruddy did not set out to replicate their designs, something, in fact, which he would do quite conspicuously a few years later at Druids Glen, a parkland course also in County Wicklow that he co-designed with Tom Craddock. Rather, he sought to celebrate their vision on the kind of grounds that both influenced and reflected their best work. The sum of the mix of extraordinary land, lessons learned, and true vision is a course that looks like it has been around for over a hundred years, not just fifteen, and that has already earned a ranking among the greatest in the world.[6]

As boldly as Patrick O'Connor declared for whom, and for whom not, Old Head was built, Pat Ruddy has done the same in describing the kind of golfing experience that visitors will find at The European Club. What awaits, says Ruddy, is *'a primeval golfing challenge'*, one that connects to the natural landscape and the origins of the game itself. **For only on a links course,** he explains, **can one witness the 'forces of the sea, the land, and the sky coming together in a convulsion of savage movement'.**[7] This is a test for 'real' golfers, Ruddy explains, those who bring skill, patience, and thought to their games. In other words, those who have the kind of game and approach to it that links golf should require.

For even the finest players, though, The European Club is a stern test. Stretching over 7,000 yards from the blue tees, the course is particularly defined by a set of par fours (none less than 389 yards, and ten of the thirteen in excess of 400) that rival any in the game. It is hard to choose a favourite among a group that has so much variety and character, yet consistency of style and shot-making demands. Ruddy's may be number seven, a monstrous par four of 470 yards usually into the teeth of the wind off Mizen Head. The hole features a narrow stream running the length of its right side and a reed-filled marsh midway up the left. The fairway alternately expands and narrows around the marsh, eventually arriving before an oval green, well guarded by swales left and back, and the ever-present water on the right. In true links fashion, especially on holes that require a long approach, the front of the green is open to a bump-and-run shot. But what a journey to get there. For its demands, explain Ruddy, involve state of mind just as importantly as state of ground or wind. This big, yet deceptively claustrophobic, hole set amidst reeds, hillocks, and valleys has earned recognition as among the best in the world.[8]

#8, The European Club, County Wicklow

Another, undoubtedly, would be the fifteenth, the last in a stretch of four beautiful and varied holes along the Irish Sea on the back nine. Although the sea can be seen, and felt, from virtually anywhere on the course, its influence is most appreciated in this stretch where the beach itself can come into play. The tee on fifteen is perched on a knob in the dunes and directs the drive to a narrow landing area between a swarm of dense, marram-covered mounds on the left and the rapidly-rising cliff on the right. The hole swings gently left at this point, completely parallel to the sea, and climbs steadily to the cliff-top green. The open, windswept placement of the green, with exhilarating views up and down the coast, is as good as it gets.

The course initially ended somewhat controversially with a small spring-fed, but artificially designed, pond surrounding the left half of the eighteenth green. But Ruddy replaced the pond in 2001 with a stream – 'acceptable water', he explains – which cuts a path across the front of the green and meanders part way up the fairway. [9] The stream is called the Jean Van de Velde Burn, after the charming French golfer who lost The Open at Carnoustie in 1999 when he dumped his third shot into the Barry Burn and took a triple bogey on the last hole. Such touches of design and homage further reveal why The European Club has earned enthusiastic reviews and a devoted following. In important ways, those reviews go beyond the course itself and speak to the links tradition that the course perpetuates. The European Club is a labour of love – a life's labour and legacy. *But it is as much about memory as it is about dreams.*

Jim Finegan, the fine American golf writer, praised Ruddy's work as 'a joyful revelation that to be great a links need not be old'. [10] Not only has The European Club demonstrated this itself, but it has influenced this awareness elsewhere. There are no finer examples of the influence of contemporary Irish links land course architecture as represented in Pat Ruddy than two courses near Bandon on Oregon's southern coast. Bandon Dunes, a design of Scotsman David Kidd, opened in 1998, and Pacific Dunes, its even more heralded twin designed by Tom

Doak, followed in 2001. Built on extraordinary links land, arguably the finest outside of the British Isles and Ireland, both courses meander through primeval grassy dunes that roll along the sweeping, wild shores of this rugged coast. '**The soul of the game resides here'**, proclaims the resort's literature, a nod to spiritual connections as well as to physical.

Not all links land layouts are great, of course. But they are unique – unique in design, location, character and, perhaps most importantly, the window they provide on the origins and nature of the game.

Wandering through the gorse and dunes-bounded valley of the seventeenth at The European Club, for example, a golfer can experience a sense of seclusion that has an eerie timelessness about it. The tempered steel or graphite-shafted club in hand is hardly a shepherd's old wooden crook.

But, in this place, in this land, it is easy to imagine the company of some ancient striker who found similar joy in launching some object towards a distant target. Links golf affords this communion.

#11, The European Club, County Wicklow

Its manifestation at The European Club provides comfort in knowing that the future of Irish golf will continue to connect to its past – *and that the gods will have another worthy place to play.*

epilogue

Why Irish Eyes Are Smiling

There is something special happening in the Emerald Isle these days. Magazines resplendent with pictorial essays and numerous websites tout the joys of travel in Ireland. The beneficiary of almost €21 billion that has come its way since joining the European Economic Community in 1973, Ireland boasts one of Europe's most successful economies. Although the recession of 2001-2002 knocked the Celtic Tiger off the double-digit economic growth rates it had posted throughout the 1990s, Ireland brims with confidence and a highly skilled, increasingly home grown, labour force. No longer a victim of a brain drain that robbed its future, Ireland is holding on to its youth and they are finding employment far from the shipyards and fields of their fathers. Chemicals and communications technology lead the turn-around – Ireland has become the world's second leading exporter of computer software – but EU subsidies and tourist spending have caused the tide to rise in all sectors of the economy. Such American corporations as Intel, Dell, Microsoft, IBM, Bristol-Myers Squibb, and Motorola have established their European base of operations in Ireland and seem settled in for the long haul.

Irish culture has never been more popular. Whether rock (U2, The Cranberries, Snow Patrol), or traditional (The Chieftains, Clannad, Mary Black) or contemporary (Enya, Sinead O'Connor, Phil Coulter), Irish music is as apt to sell out concert halls as it is to fill elevators. *Riverdance*, the high energy revue of Irish dance and music, sends several companies abroad simultaneously and has inspired a host of imitators. Celtic imagery abounds in film, whether focused on Middle Earth (*Lord of the Rings*) or distant galaxies (*Star Wars*). And books about the Irish experience and Irish characters (Patrick O'Brian's seafaring chronicles of Jack Aubrey, Frank McCourt's accounting of his own family history in *Angela's Ashes*, and *'Tis*, Seamus Heaney's poetry) regularly head bestsellers' lists.

There is no hotter city in Europe than Dublin. The 'wired generation' – half of the city's population is under 30 – has helped transform 'dear dirty Dublin' from a provincial backwater and the slum capital of Europe to a vibrant, self-confident metropolis. With its shops, restaurants, clubs, and contagious sociability, Dublin earns comparison with Prague and Budapest among the new elite of European cities. With innovative modern architecture sprouting up everywhere, the city of Swift and Shaw, Behan and Beckett, Wilde, Yeats, and Joyce has become much more than a procession of Georgian facades and smoky pubs. The latter, which number one for every 450 Dubliners, continue to define the city's gentle spirit. Yet, evidence of Continental cosmopolitanism has even appeared in these hallowed places where it is not surprising to find menus offering cappuccino and bruschetta along with pub fare standards like fish and chips and bacon and cabbage.

There are significant infrastructure challenges still to be overcome to effect balance between the old and the new, between the goal of pedestrian-friendly promenades and the reality of gridlock traffic conditions. But the best of the city's past – **its casual feel, appreciation of simple amenities like open-air cafés and vehicle-free cobblestone streets, and joyous celebration of its rich**

Wicklow Street in Dublin city centre

View through a window slit at the Rock of Cashel,
County Tipperary

cultural heritage – seems to be the template for its future. The city's apparent commitment to achieve balance in such matters leads many to believe that Dublin is both a model and a metaphor for the new Ireland.

In many respects, the same can be said about golf. **As this game is entwined with the many expressions and identities of Ireland – mythological, historical, spiritual, natural, literary – it connects the ancient and the contemporary and suggests what lays ahead for both the game and the land.**

Echoing Dublin's reputation as a 'happening' place, there is no hotter golfing destination in the world than Ireland. Several factors have contributed to this development. The success of such players as the North's Darren Clarke and the Republic's Padraig Harrington and Paul McGinley on the US and European tours have won fans for themselves and all of Ireland. The latter was particularly evident when Harrington and McGinley teamed to win the World Cup in 1997. And Irish everywhere rejoiced when Harrington won the 2007 Open in a play-off against Spain's Sergio Garcia.

The Golf Channel on television has readily brought these players and the Irish courses that host European Tour events to the attention of global viewing audiences. The designation of The K Club as the site for the Ryder Cup in 2006 and the incredible response to the Old Head course at Kinsale have emphasised the new generation of courses in Ireland, just as they have sparked a renaissance of appreciation for the older links. Anchored by Royal County Down, Ballybunion (Old), Portrush (Dunluce), and Portmarnock, rankings of the world's greatest courses regularly include a dozen or more Irish courses. With so many promising courses newly opened or under construction, including Druids Heath, Skellig Bay, and Greg Norman's much heralded Doonbeg, the Irish representation on these lists will likely increase.

What all of this adds up to is that the world's golfers, especially American and Japanese, are increasingly making

Ireland their destination of choice for a golfing holiday. The more favourable exchange rate of the euro in the Republic of Ireland over the pound in the UK helps this trend, as does, particularly with Americans after September 11, 2001, a sense that Ireland is a safe, familiar, and sufficiently exotic place to visit. That is, they have castles, ruins, natural wonders, and magical places there – and they speak English (sort of). Yet, even for the Irish, especially the 'smart' set, they are finding that they do not have to go abroad to find *haute* culture and great and varied golfing venues. They will, of course, still seek the pleasures of Lanai and Pebble Beach and Los Cabos, but choice, not necessity, will send them there. Increasingly, they may find themselves sharing rounds and draughts and updated Irish cuisine with others in their social circle – native and foreigner – at Dromoland, Adare, and Ashford.

Indeed, the once heretical notion – and secret – that Ireland is a better golfing trip than Scotland is being embraced by more and more people. The basic cost of a week long trip to Ireland, including lodging, breakfast, golf, and a rental car, is about one quarter cheaper than a similar trip to Scotland, although that is not likely to be the case for long. It is generally easier to get on Ireland's top courses than Scotland's, which often require prospective players to go through a lottery, or stay in certain hotels, or sell their first-born to have a chance. And many will argue, too, that a Smithwick's ale with a Guinness head accompanying a bowl of Irish stew are considerably easier to handle than a peaty single malt and a plate of haggis and neets. The bottom line, though, is that Ireland's top five courses – the four mentioned above plus Lahinch – may be better than Scotland's line-up of the Old Course at St Andrews, Muirfield, Turnberry (Ailsa), Royal Dornoch, and Carnoustie.

There is probably no way, or real reason, to settle a debate about whether or not the golfing experience in either of these countries exceeds that in the other. One issue is certain, though. In perhaps the most important way, that is, the place of the game in their respective sporting scenes and national cultures, golf in Ireland and Scotland compare most favourably.

The top 100 courses and championship layouts that attract well-heeled tourists and earn high ratings from *Conde Nast* are only one end of a golfing spectrum that extends from the very democratic to the most aristocratic. For far from the five star environments of The K Club, Old Head, Loch Lomond, and the Carnegie Club is a scene that underscores the extraordinary passion and appeal the game evokes. This is manifest at the numerous par three, nine-hole, and pitch and putt layouts throughout the countries. Although Ireland does not have anything quite so charming as the Children's Course in North Berwick or the public putting green on the Bruce Embankment at St Andrews, it provides ample opportunity for young people to learn the game.

Carrying starter sets or just an assortment of pared-down clubs in their hands or light bags, pre-teen boys and girls scamper across the few acres of these playing grounds, whacking shots in the general direction of their intended targets. They waste no time taking their swings or pursuing their consequences. No laboured pre-shot routines, no agonising debates over club selection, no tossing blades of grass into the air to test a breeze stiff enough to knock one over, no mummified poses plumbing putts. Nerveless haste and easy expectation characterise both the pace and practice of their play.

'The Castle', #3, Tralee Golf Club, County Kerry

A ten-year-old boy swinging his father's sawn-off, hand-me-down five iron is hardly making a political statement in the same way that his ancestors did in using golf as a symbol of irredentist patriotism after the union of England and Scotland in 1707. However unconsciously, though, he is engaged in an activity that affirms a set of values, including responsibility, self-reliance, and integrity, that are deemed important for both his community and his own well-being. These short courses and the growing calendar of junior events for both boys and girls emphasise their right of participation in a game that, through its nature and on such grounds, represents an agent of socialisation and a means for the formation of personal character.

Not just for the youth of Ireland, but for all, for every high end, guest-oriented golfing destination, there are dozens of courses offering easy access, superb playing conditions, and low green fees. From the beautifully restored Portsalon links along Ballymastocker Bay in County Donegal, to the spectacular coastal vistas of the Wicklow Golf Club high above Wicklow Bay, to the enchanting Gort Golf Club set among mature groves of holly and apple orchards near the Burren in County Galway, unpretentious clubs afford visitors, octogenarians and adolescents alike, the courtesy of their fairways and the sincerity of their hospitality.

One, in fact, would expect no less in Ireland.

This is a country that welcomes visitors into its heart.

And the heart of Ireland is the land itself. For in this beautiful, timeless and, occasionally, tortured land, there are stories to be told over and over again, and countless more yet to unfold. Golf is at home in such a land because, like no other game, it is rooted in story. Whether held in memory or in anticipation, the stories of golf are both personal and shared. They provide community among those who play the game in the present and connection both to those who wielded hickory clubs in an earlier century and to those whose first swings

have yet to occur. Like Ireland, golf's stories are woven through layers of mythology, history, spirituality, and imagination. *And hope.*

But it all comes back to the land. Ireland, of course, did not give birth to this game. Not even the *Lebor Gabala* makes that claim. But the land of Eire and Danu and Cúchulainn – and Eddie Hackett, Christy O'Connor, Chuckie O'Connell, and Pat Ruddy – has come to define it in as fully a fashion as Scotland, yet in uniquely eloquent ways, too.

For there is no place where golfers can better encounter the essential elements of the game, or become more in touch with the reasons they play it, than Ireland.

Ireland, like the game itself, blessed, vexed, and visited by the gods of myth and faith and, yes, whimsy, is a journey – and a story – that beckons.

NOTES

Introduction

1   Michael Bamberger
Sports Illustrated, 29 July 2002, G48

2   Bob Rotella
Golf Is Not a Game of Perfect
New York: Simon & Schuster, 1995

Chapter 1

1   David L. Smith, John P. Holms
The Gods of Golf
New York: Simon and Schuster, 1996

2   Michael Dames
Ireland: A Sacred Journey
New York: Barnes & Noble, 2000, *p.10*

3   Elizabeth Bowen
Bowen's Court
London: Longmans Green, 1942

4   Joseph O'Connor
The Secret World of the Irish Male
Dublin: New Island Books, 1994, *p.144*

Chapter 2

1   Quoted in Ivan Morris
Only Golf Spoken Here: Colourful Memoirs of a Passionate Irish Golfer
Chelsea, MI: Sleeping Bear Press, 2001, *p.155, p.160*

2   Carr won his first of three British Amateur championships in 1953. A ten-time Walker Cup competitor, more than any player on either side, Carr won three silver medals at the British Open as low amateur and 38 assorted Irish championships.

3   Joe Carr
"Welcome to Irish Golf"
In Louise and Rick Miracle
Trolleys and Squibs: A Golfer's Guide to Irish Links
San Francisco: Pomegranate, 2000, *p.9*

4   Donald J. Ross
Golf Has Never Failed Me
Chelsea, MI: Sleeping Bear Press, 1996, *p.198*

5   Richard Phinney and Scott Whitley
Links of Heaven: A Complete Guide to Golf Journeys in Ireland
Ogdensburg, NY: Baltray Books, 1996, *p.200*

6   John Redmond
Great Golf Courses of Ireland
Dublin: Gill & Macmillan, 1992, *p.89*

7   Louise MacNeice
Collected Poems
London: Faber, 1966

8   Phinney and Whitley
Links of Heaven, *p.34*

9   James W. Finegan
Emerald Fairways and Foam-Flecked Seas:
A Golfer's Pilgrimage to the Courses of Ireland
New York: Simon and Schuster, 1996, *p.270*

Chapter 3

1   George Peper and the Editors of *Golf Magazine*
The 500 World's Greatest Golf Holes
New York: Artisan, 2000, *p.345*

Chapter 4

1   See, for example:
O'Faolain
An Irish Journey
London: Longman and Greene, 1940;

MacNeice
"Sligo and Mayo" in **Collected Poems**
New York: Faber, 1966;

Kiely
"God's Own Country" in **Proxopera,**
A Journey to the Seven Streams
London: A.P. Watt, Ltd., 1963;

Rynne
All Ireland
London: Batsford, 1956;

Praeger
The Way That I Went
London: Hodges Figgis, 1937

2   O'Faolain
An Irish Journey

3   Derek Mahon
The Hunt By Night
New York: Oxford University Press, 1982

4   Finn MacGorman
Book of Leinster (c. 12th century)
Quoted in Dillon, Miles, Editor
Early Irish Society
Dublin: C. O. Lochlainn, 1945

5   O'Faolain
An Irish Journey

6   For a fuller introduction to his teaching
philosophy, see Fred Shoemaker
with Pete Shoemaker)
Extraordinary Golf: The Art of the Possible
(New York: Putnam, 1996

7   Quoted in Phinney and Whitley
Links of Heaven, *p.10*

8   Quoted in Redmond
Great Golf Courses of Ireland, *p.74*

In a remarkable amateur career, rivalled only by Portmarnock's Joe Carr, Burke won the Irish Open Amateur in 1947, the Irish Close Amateur eight times, the West of Ireland Amateur six times, and the South of Ireland Amateur eleven times. The latter's permanent venue is Lahinch. His championships occurred over a twenty-year period from 1928-1947. In 1932, he was named to the Walker Cup team, the first Irish golfer to be so honoured.

9   **Litany of Creation** (1575)
Quoted in Michael Dames
Ireland: A Sacred Journey
New York: Barnes & Noble, 2000, *p.244*

Chapter 5

1   Quoted in Redmond
Great Golf Courses of Ireland, *p.65*

2   Quoted in Donal Hickey
**Queen of Them All: A History of Killarney
Golf and Fishing Club, 1893-1993**
Killarney: Killarney Golf & Fishing Club, 1993, *p.29*

3   Miracle
Trolleys and Squibbs, *p.204*

4   Quoted in Finegan
Emerald Fairways and Foam-Flecked Seas, *p.189*

Chapter 6

1   See, for example:
Darwin
The Golf Courses of the British Isles
London: Duckworth and Co., 1910;
Macdonald
Scotland's Gift – Golf
New York: Scribner's, 1928;
MacKenzie
Golf Architecture
London: Simpkin, Marshall, Hamilton, Kent
and Co., 1920;

Wind
Following Through
New York: Ticknor and Fields, 1985;
Nelson
Winning Golf
New York: A.S. Barnes, 1946;
Hogan (with Herbert Warren Wind)
**Five Lessons: The Modern Fundamentals
of Golf**
New York: A.S. Barnes, 1957;
Snead
Natural Golf
New York: A.S. Barnes, 1953;
Nicklaus (with Herbert Warren Wind)
The Greatest Game of All
New York: Simon and Schuster, 1969

2   Penick (with Bud Shrake)
Harvey Penick's Little Red Book
New York: Simon and Schuster, 1992

3   Quoted in Phinney and Whitley
Links of Heaven, *p.80*

4   Ibid.

5   E. Estyn Evans
"The Irishness of the Irish" in **Ireland and the
Atlantic Heritage: Selected Writings**
Dublin: Lilliput, 1995

6   Prior to Padraig Harrington's victory in the 2007
Open, only one Irishman had ever won a professional Grand Slam event. This was Fred Daly,
who captured The Open title at Hoylake in England in 1947.

7   O'Connor (with John Redmond)
    Christy O'Connor: His Autobiography
    Dublin: Gill and Macmillan, 1985, *p.69*

8   Quoted in Brian Hewitt
    **"Christy O'Connor: The Best Player
    Never to Win a Major?"**
    Golfweek, 18 July 1998

9   O'Connor
    Autobiography, *p.11*

10 Richard MacKenzie
    **A Wee Nip at the 19th Hole: A History
    of the St. Andrews Caddie**
    Chelsea, MI: Sleeping Bear Press, 1997, *p.1-2*

11 Letter, Ruddy to Zingg
    18 August 2001
    I first met Pat Ruddy on a trip to Ireland that
    included a round at The European Club in 1995.
    We have corresponded often since than and I
    have returned to The European Club twice since
    my first round there. Pat's foreword for this
    book is a nice reflection of our friendship
    through golf.

12 Pat Ruddy
    "Evolution of the Links"
    Miracle
    Trolleys and Squibs, *p.60*

Chapter 7

1   Robert Lynd
    Home Life in Ireland
    London: Mills & Boon, 1908

2   **The Four Masters** (Trans. John O'Donovan)
    The Annals of the Kingdoms of Ireland
    Dublin: Hodges and Smith, 1851

3   Quoted in Robert Sullivan
    "A Sort of Homecoming"
    Travel & Leisure Golf, May/June 1999, *p.109*

4   Shakespeare, William
    King Lear, Act 4, Scene 1

5   Quoted in Phinney and Whitley
    Links of Heaven, *p.22-23*

6   The European Club ranked fifth behind Royal
    Portrush, Portmarnock, Royal County Down,
    and Ballybunion (Old) among Ireland's Greatest
    Courses of the Twentieth Century according
    to a 1999 poll of nationally prominent players,
    architects, golf writers, and administrators
    conducted by the Irish Golf Institute. A similar
    worldwide poll conducted by *Golfer's Companion*
    to identify the World's Greatest Courses of the
    Twentieth Century placed The European Club
    twenty-fourth. The 'youngest' course ahead
    of The European Club in the Ireland-only
    rankings was Portmarnock (1894) and, in the
    world's rankings, Pinehurst, No. 2 (1935).

7   Quoted in Miracle
Trolleys and Squibs, *p.59*

8   Peper and the Editors of *Golf Magazine*
The 500 World's Greatest Golf Holes,
p.140-141

9   Letter, Ruddy to Zingg
18 August 2001

10   Finegan
Emerald Fairways and Foam-Flecked Seas,
p.186

SOURCES

Golf

Alison, Charles S. and Colt, Harry S.
Some Essays on Golf Course Architecture
London: Country Life and George Newnes, 1920

Allen, Peter
Famous Fairways
London: Stanley Paul, 1968

Armstrong, Rob
Golfing in Ireland: The Most Complete Guide for Adventurous Golfers
Gretna, LA: Pelican, 1997

Bartlett, Michael. Editor
The Golf Book
New York: Arbor House, 1980

Callahan, Tom (with Woods, Tiger)
In Search of Tiger: A Journey Through Golf
New York: Crown, 2003

Christian, Frank (with Brown, Cal)
Augusta National and The Masters
Chelsea, MI: Sleeping Bear Press, 1996

Cook, Kevin
Tommy's Honor
New York: Gotham Books, 2007

Cornish, Geoffrey S. and Whitten, Ronald
The Architects of Golf
New York: HarperCollins, 1993
The Golf Course
New York: Rutledge, 1981

Daley, Paul. Compiler and editor
Golf Architecture: A Worldwide Perspective. 2 vols.
Gretna, LA: Pelican, 2003

Darwin, Bernard
The Golf Courses of the British Isles
London: Duckworth, 1910
A History of Golf in Britain
London: Cassell, 1952

Davies, David
"Ireland Forever"
Golf Digest, August 2002

Davis, William H., et al.
100 Greatest Courses – And Then Some
New York: Golf/Tennis, Inc., 1986

Doak, Tom
The Anatomy of a Golf Course: The Art of Golf Architecture
New York: Lyons & Burford, 1992

Doak, Tom; Scott, James S.; and Raymund M. Haddock
The Life and Work of Dr. Alister MacKenzie
Chelsea, MI: Sleeping Bear Press, 2001

Dye, Pete (with Shaw, Mark)
Bury Me in a Pot Bunker
Reading, MA: Addison Wesley, 1994

Edmund, Nick
Classic Golf Courses of Great Britain & Ireland
Boston: Little, Brown, 1997
Following the Fairways (Editor)
Hexham, England: Kensington West, 1998
"The Island: Irish Elegance From Days Gone By"
Links Magazine, March 1998
"Lahinch: Ireland's Quiet Masterpiece"
Links Magazine, September/October 1999

Fay, Michael J.
Golf, As It Was Meant To Be Played:
A Celebration of Donald Ross's Vision of the Game
New York: Universe Publishing, 2000

Fazio, Tom (with Brown, Cal)
Golf Course Designs
New York: Abrams, 2000

Finegan, James W.
Emerald Fairways and Foam-Flecked Seas:
A Golfer's Pilgrimage to the Courses of Ireland
New York: Simon and Schuster, 1996

Finn, G.A.
Lazy Days at Lahinch
Chelsea, MI: Sleeping Bear Press, 2002

Friedman, Thomas L.
"Doonbeg: Norman's Spectacular Walk
on the Moon"
Golf Digest, August 2002

Gilleece, Dermot
"Lahinch"
Links Magazine, May/June 2002

Hanse, Gil
"Recipe for a Links"
Links Magazine, July/August 2007

Haultain, Arnold
The Mystery of Golf
London: Ailsa Publishing, 1908

Hawtree, Fred
Colt and Co.
Oxford: Cambuc Archive, 1991

Hickey, Donal
Queen of Them All: A History of the Killarney
Golf and Fishing Club, 1893-1993
Killarney: Killarney Golf & Fishing Club, 1993

Hunter, Robert
The Links
New York: Scribner's, 1926

Hurdzan, Michael
Golf Course Architecture
Chelsea, MI: Sleeping Bear Press, 1996

Hutchinson, Horace
The Badminton Libary: Golf
London: Longmans, Green and Co., 1890
Fifty Years of Golf
New York: Scribner's Sons., 1919

Jones, Robert Trent, Jr.
Golf By Design
New York: Little Brown, 1993

Kirk, John and Jacobs, Timothy. Editors
The Golf Courses of Robert Trent Jones, Jr.
New York: Gallery Books, 1988

Klein, Bradley
**Discovering Donald Ross: The Architect
and His Courses**
Chelsea, MI: Sleeping Bear Press, 2001
Rough Meditations
Chelsea, MI: Sleeping Bear Press, 1997

Kroeger, Robert
The Golf Courses of Old Tom Morris
Cincinnati: Heritage Communications, 1995

Labbance, Bob
The Old Man: The Biography of Walter J. Travis
Chelsea, MI: Sleeping Bear Press, 2000

Macdonald, Charles Blair
Scotland's Gift – Golf
New York: Scribner's, 1928

MacKenzie, Alister
Golf Architecture
London: Simpkin, Marshall, Hamilton, Kent, 1920
The Spirit of St. Andrews
Chelsea, MI: Sleeping Bear Press, 1995

MacKenzie, Richard
**A Wee Nip at the 19th Hole: A History of
the St. Andrews Caddie**
Chelsea, MI: Sleeping Bear Press, 1997

Mair, Lewine
"A Great Amateur: Joe Carr"
Golf Journal, January/February 1999

McCallen, Brian
"Ballybunion, 11th Hole"
Golf Magazine, April 2000

McGuire, Brenda and John
Golf at the Water's Edge: Scotland's Seaside Links
New York: Abbeville, Press, 1997

Miracle, Louise and Rick
Trolleys and Squibs: A Golfer's Guide to Ireland
San Francisco: Pomegranate Communications, 2000

Moriarty, Jim
"The Emerald Isle Gets Greener"
Golf Digest, March 1998

Morris, Ivan
**Only Golf Spoken Here: Colourful Memoirs of
a Passionate Irish Golfer**
Chelsea, MI: Sleeping Bear Press, 2001

Murphy, Michael
Golf in the Kingdom
New York: Viking, 1972

O'Connor, Christy (with Redmond, John)
Christy O'Connor: His Autobiography
Dublin: Gill and Macmillan, 1985

Olmstead, Larry
"Golf at the Ends of the Earth"
Links Magazine, March 2003

Owen, David
"The Chosen One"
The New Yorker, 21 & 28 August 2000
The Making of the Masters
New York: Simon and Schuster, 1999

Passov, Joseph Mark
"Old Tom Morris: Golf's First True Renaissance Man"
Links Magazine, September/October 1996

Peper, George, et al.
The 500 World's Greatest Holes
New York: Artisan, 2000

Peper, George
"Origins of the Links"
Links Magazine, July/August 2007

Phinney, Richard and Whitley, Scott
Links of Heaven: A Complete Guide to Golf Journeys in Ireland
Ogdensburg, NY: Baltray Books, 1996

Price, Charles
The World of Golf
New York: Random House, 1962

Price, Robert
Scotland's Golf Courses
Edinburgh: Aberdeen University Press, 1989

Redmond, John
Great Golf Courses of Ireland
Dublin: Gill & Macmillan, 1992

Ross, Donald J.
Golf Has Never Failed Me
Chelsea, MI: Sleeping Bear Press, 1997

Rotella, Bob
Golf is Not a Game of Perfect
New York: Simon and Schuster, 1995

Rothman, Evan
"Portmarnock Golf Club"
Links Magazine, November/December 2002

Rubenstein, Lorne
A Season in Dornoch: Golf and Life in the Scottish Highlands
New York: Simon & Schuster, 2002

Rude, Jeff
"Northwest Passage"
Golfweek, 16-23 November 2002

Sampson, Curt
Hogan
Nashville: Rutledge Hill Press, 1996
The Masters: Golf, Money, and Power in Augusta, Georgia
New York: Villard, 1998

Schackleford, Geoff
The Golden Age of Golf Design
Chelsea, MI: Sleeping Bear Press, 1999
Masters of the Links: Essays on the Art of Golf and Course Design (Editor)
Chelsea, MI: Sleeping Bear Press, 1997

Seanor, Dave
"It's Better in Belfast"
Golfweek, 16-23 November 2002

Smith, David L. and Holms, John P.
The Gods of Golf
New York: Simon and Schuster, 1996

Steel, Donald
Classic Golf Links of England, Scotland, Wales and Ireland
Gretna, LA: Pelican, 1993

Steinbreder, John
"Dublin Your Pleasure"
Golfweek, 16-23 November 2002

Sullivan, Matt
"Heaven for Golfers"
Links Magazine, April 1999

Sullivan, Robert
"A Sort of Homecoming"
Travel & Leisure Golf, May/June 1999

Sutton, Martin H. F. Editor
The Book of the Links
London: W. H. Smith & Sons, 1912

Thomas, George C., Jr.
Golf Architecture in America: Its Strategy and Construction
Los Angeles: Times Mirror Press, 1927
Sleeping Bear Press reprint, 1997

Thomson, Peter
"Call of the Wild"
Links Magazine, July/August 2007

Ward-Thomas, Pat. Editor
The World Atlas of Golf
London: Mitchell Beazley, 1976

Wethered, H. N. and Simpson, Tom
The Architectural Side of Golf
Worcestershire: Grant Books, 1995
Facsimile of 1929 edition

Williams, Jeff
"Doonbeg"
Links Magazine, March 2003
"Waterville"
Links Magazine, November/December 2000

Wind, Herbert Warren
Following Through
New York: Ticknor and Fields, 1985
"Understanding Golf Course Architecture"
Golf Digest, November 1966

Zingg, Paul J.
A Good Round: A Journey Through the Landscapes and Memory of Golf
Danbury, CT: Rutledge, 1999
"Myth, History and the Sense of Place"
The Journal of the Shivas Irons Society,
Spring 2004

Irish Culture, History and Mythology

Arensberg, Conrad
The Irish Countryman
Cambridge: Harvard University Press, 1937

Ashe, Geoffrey
Land to the West
London: Collins, 1962

Bacon, Francis
"Of Gardens" (1601)
London: John Lane, 1902 reprint

Barker, Ernest
Ireland in the Last Fifty Years
Oxford: Clarendon, 1917

Bazin, Germain
Paradeisos: The Art of the Garden
Boston: Little, Brown, 1988

Berrall, Julia S.
The Garden: An Illustrated History
New York: Viking, 1966

Boll, Heinrich. Trans. Leila Vennewitz
Irish Journal
Chicago: Northwestern University Press, 1994

Bowen, Elizabeth
Bowen's Court
London: Longmans Green, 1942

Brown, Terence
Ireland: A Social and Cultural History
New York: Harper Collins, 1981

Cahill, Thomas
How the Irish Saved Civilization
New York: Doubleday, 1995

Connolly, S. F.
The Oxford Companion to Irish History
New York: Oxford University Press, 1998

Cosgrove, Art
Late Medieval Ireland, 1370-1541
Dublin: Edco, 1996

Cotter, Claire
"Atlantic Fortifications – The Duns of the Aran Islands"
Archaeology Ireland, VIII, 1, 1994

Craig, Patricia. Editor
The Oxford Book of Ireland
New York: Oxford University Press, 1998

Cronin, Mike
A History of Ireland
New York: Palgrave, 2000

Curran, Bob
A Field Guide to Irish Fairies
San Francisco: Chronicle Books, 1998

Daly, Mary
Social and Economic History of Ireland
Dublin: Edco, 1981

Dames, Michael
Ireland: A Sacred Journey
New York: Barnes & Noble, 2000

Dillon, Myles
Early Irish Literature
Chicago: University of Chicago Press, 1948
Early Irish Society (Editor)
Dublin: C. O. Lochlainn, 1945

Duffy, Sean. Editor and contributor
Atlas of Irish History
New York: Macmillan, 1997
The Concise History of Ireland
Dublin: Gill & Macmillan, 2000

Flanagan, Laurence
Ancient Ireland: Life Before the Celts
Dublin: Gill & Macmillan, 2000

Foster, Roy F.
The Irish Story: Telling Tales and Making It Up in Ireland
New York: Oxford University Press, 2003
Modern Ireland, 1600-1972
London: Penguin, 1990

Four Masters. Trans. John O'Donovan
The Annals of the Kingdom of Ireland
Dublin: Hodges and Smith, 1851

George, Michael and Bowe, Patrick
The Gardens of Ireland
Boston, Little, Brown, 1986

Harris, Nathaniel
Heritage of Ireland: A History of Ireland and Its People
New York: Checkmark Books, 1998

Heaney, Marie
Over Nine Waves: A Book of Irish Legends
London: Faber and Faber, 1994

Heath, Ian and Sque, David
The Irish Wars, 1485-1603
London: Reed International Books, 1993

Herity, Michael and Eogan, George
Ireland in Prehistory
London: Routledge & Kegan Paul, 1977

Herm, Gerhard
The Celts: The People Who Came Out of the Darkness
New York: St. Martin's Press, 1977

Hewitt, John
The Collected Poems of John Hewitt
London: Blackstaff, 1966

Jackson, Alvin
Ireland, 1798-1998: Politics and War
Oxford: Blackwell, 1999

Jones, Carleton
Temples of Stone: Exploring The Megalithic Tombs of Ireland
Cork: The Collins Press, 2007

Jones, Kathy
The Ancient British Goddesses: Her Myths,
Legends and Sacred Sites
Somerset, England: Ariadne Publications, 2000

Kinsella, Thomas. Editor
The Tain
London: Oxford University Press, 1969

Koch, John T.
The Celtic Heroic Age
Andover, MA: Celtic Studies Publications, 1994

Larner, Jim. Editor
Killarney – History and Heritage
Cork: The Collins Press, 2005

Lydon, James
The Making of Ireland: From Ancient
Times to the Present
London: Routledge, 1998

Lynch, Ann
"Poulnabrone – A Stone in Time"
Archaeology Ireland, VII, 3, 1988

Lyons, David
Land of the Poets: Ireland
London: PRC Publishing, 2002

Macalister, Robert A. E.
Lebor Gabala Erenn
Dublin: Educational Co. of Ireland, 1938

MacKillop, James
Dictionary of Celtic Mythology
New York: Oxford University Press, 1998

MacNeice, Louis
Collected Poems
London: Faber, 1966

MacNiovaill, Gearoid
Ireland Before the Vikings
Dublin: Gill & Macmillan, 1972

McCullough, David W.
Wars of the Irish Kings
New York: Crown, 2000

Miller, Kerby A.
Emigrants and Exiles: Ireland and the Irish
Exodus to North America
New York: Oxford University Press, 1985

Morgan, Hiram
Tyrone's Rebellion
Woodbridge, Suffock: Royal Historical Society/
Boydell and Brewer, 1993

Morton, H. V.
In Search of Ireland
London: Methuen, 1930

Moryson, Fynes
An Itinerary
Glasgow: James MacLehose and Sons, 1908

Murphy, Gerard
Saga and Myth in Ancient Ireland
Cork: Mercier Press, 1961

Nairn, Richard and Crowley, Miriam
Wild Wicklow: Nature in the Garden of Ireland
Dublin: TownHouse, 1998

O'Brien, Jacqueline and Harbison, Peter
**Ancient Ireland: From Prehistory to the
Middle Ages**
New York: Oxford University Press, 1996

O'Corrain, Donncha
Ireland Before the Normans
Dublin: Gill & Macmillan, 1972

O'Driscoll, Robert. Editor
The Celtic Consciousness
New York: George Braziller, 1981

Ó hÓgáin, Dáithí
Historic Ireland: 5000 Years of Ireland's Heritage
Dublin: Gill & Macmillan, 2000

O'Kelly, M. J.
Early Ireland
Cambridge: Cambridge University Press, 1989

O Nuallain, Sean
"**The Megalithic Tombs of Ireland: Neolithic
Tombs and Their Art**"
Expedition, XX1, 3, September 1979

Powers, Alice Leccese. Editor
Ireland in Mind: An Anthology
New York: Vintage, 2000

Praeger, Robert Lloyd
Natural History of Ireland
London: Collins, 1950

Raffaelli, Laure; Simon, Odil; and Rousselet,
Sabine, Editors
Ireland
New York: Knopf, 1995

Schama, Simon
Landscape and Memory
New York: Knopf, 1995

Scherman, Katharine
**The Flowering of Ireland: Saints, Scholars
and Kings**
Boston: Little, Brown, 1981

Sjoestedt, Marie-Louise. Trans. Dillon, Myles
Gods and Heroes of the Celts
Dublin: Four Courts Press, 1994

Smyth, Daragh
A Guide to Irish Mythology
Dublin: Irish Academic Press, 1986

Stewart, A. T. Q.
The Narrow Ground: Aspects of Ulster, 1609-1969
Belfast: Blackstaff, 1997

Synge, J. M.
The Aran Islands
Dublin: Maunsel & Roberts, 1921

Thacker, Christopher
The History of Gardens
Berkeley: University of California Press, 1979

Tourtellot, Jonathan B. Editor
Discovering Britain and Ireland
Washington, D.C.: National Geographic
Society, 1985

Zuccelli, Christine
**Stones of Adoration: Sacred Stones and Mystic
Megaliths of Ireland**
Cork: The Collins Press, 2007

Photography

Eric B. Johnson
front cover, introduction page, p.11, p.20, p.23, p.32, p.37, p. 41, p.44, p.51, p.56, p.58, p.61, p.69, p.75, p.76, p.79, p.82, p.87, p.95, p.96, p.103, p.104, p.117, p.133, p.141, p.146, p.147, p.163, p.164, p.168, p.190, p.191

Courtesy of Royal County Down Golf Club
p.54

Larry Lambrecht
p.73

Courtesy of Killarney Golf and Fishing Club
p.109

Courtesy of Druids Glen Golf Club
p.112

Courtesy of Royal Dublin Golf Club
p.124, p.129

Courtesy of Pat Ruddy
p.136

Courtesy of Old Head Golf Links
p.144, p.151

Courtesy of The European Club
p.155, p.158

Greenside bunker, #10, The Island Club, County Dublin

Biographies

PAUL J. ZINGG

Paul is the President of California State University, Chico, and a Professor of History. He is the author of several books on American history and sport, including two widely acclaimed works on baseball – *Harry Hooper: An American Baseball Life* (1993, second edition: 1994) and *Runs, Hits, and an Era: The Pacific Coast League, 1903-1958* (1994). His books on golf include: *A Good Round: A Journey Through the Landscapes and Memory of Golf* (1999) and *The Moraine Country Club, 1930-2005* (2005).

ERIC B. JOHNSON

Eric is a Professor of Photography and Digital Imaging in the Department of Art and Design, California Polytechnic State University in San Luis Obispo, California.

KATHRYN E. MCCORMICK

Katie is the Principal and Creative Director of McCormick Design in San Luis Obispo, California, and an Assistant Professor of Graphic Design in the Department of Art and Design, California Polytechnic State University in San Luis Obispo, California.

Paul Zingg with Michael 'Chuckie' O'Connell, Tralee Golf Club, County Kerry, in 2002

production notes

This book was designed and packaged by McCormick Design, San Luis Obispo, California. *(Special thanks to Zachary Charles and Renée Lowe.)* Photographs are by Eric B. Johnson, Larry Lambrecht and acquired from golf clubs, as noted. The text was set in Adobe Janson. Special thanks to Bradley Klein, Pat Ruddy, and Katie McCormick for editing the drafts. The printing was done in Italy by L.E.G.O. S.p.A.. The paper is 130gsm matt coated wood free.